ıssian

D0762388

EUROPE IN THE RUSSIAN MIRROR
FOUR LECTURES IN ECONOMIC HISTORY

EUROPE IN THE RUSSIAN MIRROR

FOUR LECTURES IN ECONOMIC HISTORY

BY

ALEXANDER GERSCHENKRON

Professor of Economics, Harvard University

CAMBRIDGE
AT THE UNIVERSITY PRESS
1970

Published by the Syndics of the Cambridge University Press
Bentley House, 200 Euston Road, London, N.W.1
American Branch: 32 East 57th Street, New York, N.Y. 10022

Library of Congress Catalogue Card Number: 76–96090
Standard Book Number 521 07721 4

Set in Great Britain by R. and R. Clark, Ltd., Edinburgh
and printed in the United States of America

To the memory of
THOMAS JAMES WILSON

Ex umbris alienis lux

CONTENTS

PREFACE

The following four Ellen McArthur Lectures were deli-
vered at Cambridge University in May 1968. In revising
the manuscript for publication I made a number of altera-
tions, both stylistic and substantive, and a good many
additions, but I did not try to change the tone of an oral
presentation. To do so would have seduced me into an
attempt to produce a much more comprehensive treatise
of the subject, which is something I hope to reserve for
another time. It remains for me to express my gratitude
to the seminar which met after the last lecture and whose
members offered stimulating strictures, and beyond that
to the hospitality of the academic community of Cambridge and, above all, to Pembroke College which was
my host during that wonderful fortnight of the English
spring, which convinced me that it could have been
nothing but the requirements of the meter that made
Browning change May to April.

I should also like to state my appreciation to the Institute for Advanced Study in Princeton and its director,
Carl Kaysen, for providing a year of freedom from academic duties and with it, among other things, the leisure
to transform the original draft of these lectures—a task
that was greatly facilitated by the competent assistance
supplied by my secretary at the Institute, Mrs Anna
Maria Holt.

A. G.

Cambridge, Massachusetts
June 1969

1

The title of this series of lectures is broad and ambitious. Their actual subject matter is much more narrow and much more modest. Essentially, I should like to show what light, if any, is cast by the study of Russian economic history on some selected issues that have preoccupied students of Western economic history. This is a rather specific problem, to be illustrated by a couple of special cases. Yet, in dealing with it, I cannot avoid raising the question of what for want of a less heavy term may be called Europeanization of Russian economic history, thus placing the problem within a much wider framework and seeing it as an integral part of the old dichotomy: Russia and Europe, or rather Russia versus Europe.

Let me begin by saying that historically seen Russia was first and foremost a geographical concept and an ambiguous one at that. What was the landlocked mass of the immense Russian plains east of the Ural Mountains? Was it the backyard of Europe, or perhaps the wasteland behind Europe's backyard? Was it Europe at all? True, when I was a pupil in a Russian gymnasium more than half a century ago, we were taught that there was definitely such a thing as European Russia, the Ural Mountains being half in Europe and half in Asia, whereas the Caucasus surprisingly enough turned out to be altogether in Asia. But Russian secondary schools were so atrociously bad that no one who spent his years there in a state of what Harold Laski in his favored phrase used to call 'a dull and resentful coma' could possibly take seriously any knowledge dispensed in those institutions of unlearning. By contrast, an average Russian traveler of the nineteenth or early twentieth century, leaving for a trip abroad, had no difficulty in giving an unconscious but very definite answer to the question. Quite naturally, he would announce that he 'was going to Europe'. And at the border, after the Russian gendarme, a look of grave suspicion on his face, had completed his close scrutiny of the passport in the dingy, ill-smelling customs hall and the 'European' train with its narrower gauge had crossed the dividing bridge on which the double-headed and the single-headed eagles faced each other in hostile silence, then looking out of the window and watching the neat red-roofed houses of the Prussian villages, the beautiful ribbons of the roads, and the well-fed cattle in the pastures, struck by the enormous contrast, the traveler would exclaim with admiring envy or murmur with envious contempt: 'Europe! this is Europe.'

But behind these ingrained habits of speech and thought stood a large body of Russian intellectual history, with its perennial concern with the problem of Russia versus Europe. For and against Europe the struggle went on. To some, Russia versus Europe meant a divinely anointed autocrat versus venal parliamentarians; orthodoxy, that is, true Christianity, versus catholicism, protestantism, and agnosticism; God versus Mammon; idealism versus materialism; generosity and warm-heartedness versus cold rationalism; communal institutions, mutual aid, and social justice versus rugged individualism and egotism; the blessings of peasant life, the good life in Christ, versus the cancer of proletarianism and the depravity of city life. For very different reasons and with great variations in emphasis and ingredients those anti-European attitudes were shared by reactionary servants of the absolutist monarchy, passionate Slavophiles, disenchanted Westerners[1] who still abhorred autocracy, and by many radicals who saw the germinating of a promise of a just and good society in the Russian *mir* and the Russian *artel*.

2

To others, Russia versus Europe meant superstition and ignorance, violence and coarseness, misery, dirt and stagnation, and above all un-freedom versus enlightenment, cleanliness, self-discipline, foresight, welfare, progress, and liberty. At times, a pro-European, a Westerner, would claim that with the Petrine reforms Russia had committed itself irreversibly, to which an 'Anti-European' would retort that the Petrine reforms had produced nothing but a thin veneer over Russian substance. But essentially and for a long time both groups would agree on one thing: Russia was not Europe or not yet Europe and the debate revolved around the question whether it should become Europe or remain Russia. That is to say, if we leave aside the aspirations of the extremists who dreamt of a Europe reformed and ennobled by the spirit of Holy Russia; the Soviet policies after 1917 being only a new, though much more virulent, incarnation of Russian Messianism. (Those who should wonder about Russian Messianism based on a Western ideology might consider that in some respects also the spirit of the Church in Holy Russia was a perverted form of Christianity just as Soviet ideology is a perverted form of Marxism.)

It was in the closing decades of the last century that the old discord reached its peak, transformed both in emphasis and in the character of the participants. It was now in the main a debate within a socialist camp, and its scope was greatly limited. Religious, philosophical, to some extent, even political aspects of the problem had receded into the background. What remained and was discussed with an unprecedented degree of concentration was the economic problem. In the parlance of the period the question was: Was Russia on her road to socialism to pass through the stage of capitalism or could she 'skip that stage' and establish a socialist system based on the previously mentioned indigenous Russian institutions? It was the Russian Marxists, or 'the Russian disciples of Marx' as they called themselves (which sounded more

scholarly and afforded some protection against the watch-
ful but often naïve censors), who took the 'pro-capitalist'
line; and it was the populists, the descendants of the
radicals of the sixties who advocated the 'Russian' way.

This is not the place to dwell on the various curiosities
of the debate. I have done it elsewhere at some length.[2]
Suffice it to mention two things. First: the populists, too,
knew their Marx and managed to deduce from Marxian
theory the irrefutable 'proof' that, for purely economic
reasons, capitalism, that is the modern industrial system,
was doomed to fail in Russia; while the disciples of Marx
offered the equally incontrovertible proposition that by
virtue of inexorable economic laws Russia was bound 'to
pass through the stage of capitalism'. And second: despite
the high level of the debate and the great polemical skill
of the participants; despite the fact that in its course
much useful material was presented on the contemporaneous economic conditions in the country, it was little
more than shadow boxing. In the decade of the 1890s
when the logomachy attained the acme of passion, Russia
found herself in the middle of a great spurt of industrialization, and the hotly-debated question had been im-
pressively resolved by the actual flow of events. It is, of
course, not a solitary example of intellectual history
lagging behind economic history. The controversies between Malthus and Ricardo, or Sismondi and Say, and,
even more strikingly, between the opponents and advo-
cates of the 'industrial state' in Germany (the latter
conducted of all times in the early years of this century)
—all these belong in the same chapter and tell the same
story. This, however, does not mean that the controversies of this type were nothing but illusions and delusions.
The stand taken by the disciples of Marx in Russia performed a clear function. By emerging so clearly victorious
from the conflict, Russian Marxism of the period rendered
possible an acceptance of modern economic development
by the intelligentsia and, paradoxically enough, provided

vindication and stimulation to the hated autocratic government in its policies of rapid industrialization. By showing that modern industrialization was inevitable, Russian Marxism supplied a strong impetus to practical action designed to make it 'inevitable'.

In the process, however, something else was accomplished which bears more directly on the subject matter of these lectures. The great debate aroused a lively interest in the economic and social history of the country. It seemed important to show that also in the past, in the rather remote past, Russian developments displayed basic similarities with European development. True, the winds of Renaissance and Reformation died down before reaching the steppes and forests of the East. The age of westward and southward discoveries, if anything, moved Russia farther away from Europe, and hardly touched the country, except perhaps for the belated effect of the influx of precious metals; which, incidentally, feeble as it was, affected the structure of relative prices in a way that was well in line with what had been occurring in Europe.[3] All the more significant, therefore, was an interesting and illuminating attempt to destroy the belief that Russia had never known anything resembling European feudalism. N. P. Pavlov-Sil'vanskii in his original studies (beginning in 1897) was able to trace a number of institutions which more or less closely duplicated those in existence in the West, particularly in France. He found it possible to speak of *beneficia*, commendations, fiefs, immunities, both judicial and administrative as well as taxative, of *servitium* and *obsequium*, of vassals and sub-vassals, and of specific obligations of servile status, such as for marriage, as existing in Russia of the period between the thirteenth and fifteenth centuries.[4]

In some respects, Pavlov-Sil'vanskii's pioneering investigations have retained their value to this day. But later studies, no doubt, stressed a good many features relating to differences rather than similarities between

Russia and the Occident. Neither the rising of vassals to the position of sovereign lords nor the concept of mutual loyalty—Max Weber's *Treuepflichten* or Marc Bloch's *contrat bilatéral d'obéissance et de protection*,[5] so much emphasized as essential for the spirit of feudalism—was said to be characteristic of Russian history. The Russian boyar's right of free departure [*vol'nyi ot'ezd*] was indeed inconsistent with Western feudalism, and it was abolished in a period which Pavlov-Sil'vanskii considered as being no longer feudal. The same is probably true of the peasants' right to leave the estate [*otkaz*] which Pavlov-Sil'vanskii all too readily identified with *le droit de désaveu*; the *otkaz*, too, was eliminated in a subsequent period.[6] In fact, viewing the whole flow of Russian history much more fundamental differences can be found. Still, Marc Bloch, who had little interest in Russia, still cited Emperor Nicholas I's statement about the 100,000 estate owners being his police chiefs as peculiar to feudalism—and this in the nineteenth century rather than the fourteenth or fifteenth centuries.[7] However that may be, within the context of the period, Pavlov-Sil'vanskii's work offered, even though somewhat belatedly, a further corroboration for the one side of the debate. If the European development had proceeded from feudalism to capitalism and if, as befitted the intellectual habits of the period, this sequence was to be considered an unmalleable iron law of development, then it was clear that by virtue of the same law Russia could not possibly escape capitalism. Bold inferential leaps of this sort are not necessarily in the best scholarly tradition, but there is little doubt that they played their part in providing much needed ideological grease for the wheels of the nascent industrial system.

To mention another type of valuable contribution to Russian economic history that was generated by the debate I may refer to Tugan-Baranovskii's monograph on *Russian Factory*,[8] the first modern study of the industrial history of the country. Tugan-Baranovskii, probably the most original Russian economist, was amazingly broad in his interests: his contributions to economics comprised value theory and theory of distribution, the theory of business cycles, where he has left a permanent mark, and the theory of markets, to say nothing of a theory of the cooperative movement and a critique of Marxism. The theory of markets, incidentally, offers a fascinating example of the insularity in the development of economic thought. While in England Keynes could quite plausibly regard all his predecessors as committed to the acceptance of Say's law, Tugan-Baranovskii presented a different view: after the criticism of Say's law by Sismondi, Tugan argued, it fell into general disrepute; but he, Tugan-Baranovskii, was to show that it was an altogether reasonable proposition as he proceeded to do with the help of an investment for investment model; thus trying to confound those who expected Russian capitalism to founder in the shallows of insufficient aggregate demand. Tugan-Baranovskii's study on the Russian factory described effectively the vicissitudes of Russian industrial history in the nineteenth century—with some retrospects into the eighteenth century—stressing both the advances made but also the various obstacles that, until the most recent time, had obstructed industrial progress. As far as the political and ideological motivation went, *mutatis mutandis* Tugan-Baranovskii certainly would have liked to arrive with regard to industrial history at the same results as Pavlov-Sil'vanskii with regard to feudalism. But Tugan-Baranovskii was a serious scholar. It was left, therefore, to Soviet historians to discover an industrial revolution in Russia in the reign of Nicholas I and to bolster such views by reviving Tarle's old 1910 shocker, the assertion, that is, that Russia even in the last quarter of the eighteenth century was by no means a backward country economically speaking.[9]

One may add parenthetically that Soviet economic

historians still could not break out of the charmed circle of the old debate. They had still to go on proving the case for Russian capitalism; and since in the 1890s the Marxian tendency was to stress and overstress the disintegration of the Russian field commune, the *obshchina*, the relevant Soviet literature has sought to avoid discussing the *obshchina* as a retarding factor in Russian industrialization. As said before, intellectual history at times tends to move behind the times; under a dictatorial regime—as likely as not—it begins to execute what in Russian military drill is called *shag na meste*—step on the spot—which is perhaps more graphic than the equivalent English command 'mark time', and at any rate is a rather noisy activity and a form of locomotion that does not lead you very far.

On closer look, Russian economic history as it emerged either from Pavlov-Sil'vanskii or from Tugan-Baranovskii was not a faithful replica of the economic history of Europe. Naturally not. The historical reality was a good deal more complex than it appeared to the participants of Russian debates. The latter tended to ignore both the existence not of one but of several 'Europes' as well as that of varying degrees of differences and similarities between Russia and those 'Europes'. And this is probably fortunate from the point of view of the main concern of these lectures. If Russian economic history were merely a faithful duplication of some synthetic image of its European counterpart; or, alternatively, if Russian economic history were altogether *sui generis*, it would have been futile to hope to receive from it much enlightenment of interesting and significant aspects of European economic history. To be sure, something still could be said in a very general fashion. Marc Bloch in stressing the importance of Western security against foreign inroads invited his readers to consider 'for a moment what Russian history would have been like without the Mongolian invasion'.[10] This is an interesting example showing

8

that a great historian may be quite willing to indulge in counter-factual history and should be kept in mind by those historians who oppose excursions into history in the conditional mood on the part of modern economic historians' as allegedly incompatible with the canons of historical research. And it is primarily with the Mongolian invasion in mind that one must speak, as I have done, of Russia as a geographic concept. But following this line of thought surely would not lead far beyond a few generalities. To penetrate at least somewhat deeper into the problem I propose to discuss two specific questions—what can Russian economic history teach us with regard to:

1) Max Weber's hypothesis concerning protestant ethics and the spirit of capitalism;

2) the phenomenon of mercantilism?

Thereafter I shall return to the broader problem.

It cannot be my purpose here to plunge into a discussion of the voluminous body of literature which arose from Max Weber's seminal idea.[11] Weber himself presented it in a tentative, qualified, almost playful way. It was not for nothing that he liked from time to time to refer expressly to the 'play impulse'[12] in scholarly work. This, however, had not been the spirit in which Weber's suggestive supposition has been treated and is being treated in a broad segment of the relevant literature. There, the reservations and qualifications with which Weber surrounded his thesis have been cast to the winds, and the hypothesis—no more than a program for research —has been accepted as an unshakably established truth. In the middle, occupying a moderate position, stand those who have claimed that there was indeed a connection between protestantism and capitalism, but that the causal nexus must be tied the other way, protestantism being viewed as a natural ideology to have been espoused by those who were engaged in 'capitalist' activities for reasons that had nothing to do with any religion; or by those who, as for example Werner Sombart, claim that both 'capitalism and protestantism were produced by the same new spirit [*neuer Geist*]'.[13] By contrast, Kurt Samuelsson,[14] the Swedish scholar and the author of the most recent contribution to the subject, has denied that the hypothesis had any merit at all. He refused to consider the direction of the causation and bluntly rejected the existence of any connection.

It is not my business here to discuss the merits and demerits of the positions taken and to examine the validity of the points made. For the purposes of this presentation I wish to neglect altogether the very existence of this literature. What solely interests me at present is the following: Max Weber claimed that it was the doctrines of Calvinism that created the spirit of capitalism, and he traced the rather twisty road that is supposed to have led from predestination and unconditional election—the melancholy tidings that just as well might have caused despair and passivity—to the duty to believe oneself chosen and to attain the corroboration of that belief and with it the certainty of salvation by worldly activity in one's calling while rejecting the idle pleasures of the world. The result was a rational system of worldly asceticism with its specific stress on industry and frugality, honesty and prudence, and positive attitude toward money and acquisition of wealth—in short the capitalistic spirit, and with it the origins of modern capitalism. The origins! For time and again Max Weber stresses the temporal limits of the connection. The modern situation, he felt, was profoundly different:

'The capital system so needs this devotion to the calling of making money, it is an attitude towards material goods which is so well suited to that system, so intimately bound up with conditions of survival in the economic struggle for existence, that there can today no longer be any question of a necessary connection of that acquisitive manner of life with any single *Weltanschauung*.'[15]

It is perhaps regrettable that Weber elsewhere in his essay did not resist the temptation to refer to contemporaneous conditions in Germany in the light of his thesis and thus to weaken his qualification. And equally regrettable is the use of the word 'necessary' in the sentence just quoted. Historical necessity is, of course, a meaningless term, a circumstance Weber understood better than anybody else. It is such unguarded use that has made it possible for ardent admirers of Weber's thesis to become so apodictic in their presentations thereof. The truth, of course, is that far from being able to ascertain the necessity of a connection—except in a definitional sense—we are also unable in dealing with problems of this sort to provide anything that can be regarded as proofs of a given thesis. Much as I believe in the virtue of quantitative research, I doubt that in this case any attempt to explore a large number of countries with the help of regression analysis would produce much enlightenment. The conditions in each case are shot through with individual peculiarities, and the variables to be used would be uncertain indeed. All we can do is to establish, by looking at an individual case, the degree of plausibility which appears inherent in such a thesis and to see whether the result satisfies our sense of reasoned adequacy. And this is precisely what I intend to do here. I should like to test the plausibility of the causal connection between a theological doctrine and economic activities by exploring an area far removed from the West and in the case of a religious persuasion altogether alien to the doctrines of Calvin and Calvinist theologists. I am referring to the case of the Russian Old Believers. As will be made clear presently, this case possesses some very special features which make it particularly, and perhaps uniquely, suitable for the purpose at hand.

The salient points in the history of the schism in the Russian Church are well known and can be quickly retold. The Mongolian domination and the shift of Russian

11

statehoods northward, away from Kiev, had tended to isolate the Russian Church from the Byzantine source of its theology. After the Florentine Union of Byzantium with Rome (1439) and the conquest of Constantinople by the Turks (1453) some doubts began to be cast on the orthodoxy of the Greek Church, while Muscovy's increased power and self-esteem generated the theory, or rather the idea, of the Third Rome and counseled a certain deliberate withdrawal from Greek tutelage. Still the uneasy feeling of Russian inferiority in matters of ecclesiastic learning could not be suppressed altogether. In the long years of isolation and the concomitant decline of learning many an error of translating from the Greek and of copying Church-Slavonic manuscripts had crept into the holy texts. The copyists were unreliable. The lazy copyists used to omit words, the eager ones used to invent additions, and the ignorant ones simply garbled. Moreover, deviations in rituals from those used in the Greek Church had developed. Some of those deviations occurred because of changes within Russia; others because of changes abroad.

As early as the beginning of the sixteenth century, attempts were made to correct the errors and to attain conformity in the rituals. A learned monk, Maxim the Greek, educated in Italian universities, was called to undertake the corrections. It was an ill-starred enterprise. Maxim knew no Russian or Church-Slavonic; his co-workers in Moscow knew no Greek. Accordingly, Maxim translated Greek texts into Latin and the Russians then translated his Latin into Church-Slavonic. In the event, Maxim was banned to a monastery, and later on the Council of 1551 in the Hundred Chapters of its Canon —the so-called *Stoglav*—solemnly reaffirmed the ancient rituals. In particular it rejected the triple hallelujah (Chapter 42), declared shaving of beards a Latin heresy (Chapter 40), and pronounced anathema on making the sign of the cross 'with three fingers'—another Latin

12

heresy (Chapter 21). For the rest, negligent copyists were threatened with severe punishment (Chapter 28).[16] The decision of the Council did not mean that the problem was dead and buried. The impact left by Maxim the Greek was considerable, as was revealed by his relatively very early canonization (1591),[17] a couple of years after Moscow's immensely increased status was confirmed by the establishment of his own patriarchate. At any rate, a century after the *Stoglav* the situation had changed radically.

The expansion of the Russian state southward, the acquisition of the Ukraine on the left bank of the River Dnieper, in particular the acquisition of Kiev (1667) which had preserved much of the ecclesiastic learning, had raised the problem of the western Ukraine and Belorussia—still under the Polish rule—and therewith the delicate question of the Uniate Church, established in 1596 by the Brest Union, in which the Orthodox Church had recognized the supremacy of the Pope. The southward movement was to bring Russia into direct contact with the Turks and created the lure of further expansion into Danubian and Trans-Danubian areas whose populations were Greek Orthodox. In fact, in the middle of the seventeenth century a leading Moscow statesman spoke of expansion to the very shores of the Adriatic.

Thereby, a crucial landmark was reached in the long process of territorial growth which eventually transformed the Duchy of Moscow—originally a good deal smaller than present-day Belgium—into an empire covering one-sixth of the globe and reaching far westward into central Europe. At that point, conformity with the Greek Church in text and ritual became an important element of the country's foreign policies and aspirations. The religious provincialism of Moscow could be maintained no longer. The withdrawal was followed by the return. Accordingly, the reform, or rather the adjustments, were to come. The State decided and the Church obeyed.[18] It did so half willingly and half reluctantly.

For the Church was vulnerable from both sides: the lower clergy and beyond it the masses of the faithful on the one hand and the State on the other. Nikon, the strong-minded Patriarch (since 1652), wanted indeed to carry out the corrections of the holy texts, and the printing press had made such corrections more urgent than ever. He might have relaxed on the question of rituals (which at least once in a private conversation he declared to be unimportant).[19] But publicly he was unable to tolerate any opposition which detracted from the authority of the Church at a moment when this authority was gravely threatened by the encroachment of the State. In the end, Nikon lost to both sides. He became the arch-fiend in the eyes of the Old Believers and he first retired into voluntary exile and then was formally deposed as Patriarch and sent to a monastery in the far north by the same Council (1666/7) at which the traditional rituals were as solemnly anathematized as had been the projected innovations some hundred years earlier, and at which the ordinances laid down in the *Stoglav* were declared to be null and void.[20] And this was the origin of the Great Schism in the Russian Church separating the official, State-protected and State-dominated Church from the Old Believers who refused to part with the old ways that had been sanctified by the custom of centuries.

Let me mention briefly the most important points at issue. The Old Believers or Schismatics—*Raskol'niki*, as they were officially described by Church and State, believed:

1) that the sign of the cross should be made with two outstretched fingers (index and middle finger) rather than with three fingers (thumb, index and middle finger) held together;

2) that the hallelujah in the doxology—the praise of

14

the Lord—should be chanted twice and not thrice; and that in Church-Slavonic the words 'Glory to thee, Oh Lord' rather than the words 'Praise the Lord' should be added;

3) that the name of Jesus (*Isus*) should be spelled and pronounced with one 'I' rather than two 'Is', the second 'I' transliterating the Greek letter 'eta';

4) that processions around the church should move clockwise ('with the sun') rather than counter-clockwise ('against the sun');

5) that crosses on churches, tombs, etc. must have eight ends rather than six or four;

6) that in accordance with 'the doctrine of three trees' crosses on churches must be made of certain types of timber only;

7) that rosaries should be used in prayer also by laymen, and that such rosaries must be made of leather;

8) the use of seven rather than five hosts in the Eucharist.

Various discrepancies in the holy texts could be added to the preceding list, a good many of them deriving from mis-translations, as, for instance, the use of the words in the Creed: 'Holy Ghost . . . whose Kingdom has no end' as against 'Holy Ghost . . . whose Kingdom *will be* without end'; or a difference in the reference to Jesus in the Kyrie eleison petition. It is, however, safe to say that none of these discrepancies would change in any way the basic conclusion that must be drawn inescapably: no doctrinal point of any substantive significance reflecting perceptible difference in the conception of the world was involved in the Schism.

Soviet historiography, anxious also in this area to demonstrate the uniform character of Russian and Western history, went to some pains in order to discover a 'Reformation movement' in Russia between the fourteenth century and the first half of the sixteenth century.[21] Indeed, in the ecclesiastic debates of that period a good deal was said of the corruption of the clergy. Simony—

15

'preferment upon graft'—and acquisition of land by the monasteries were criticized. There were some traces intimating discussion of original sin, election, and grace. The concept of 'autarchy' [*samovlast'e*] was mentioned and is now interpreted to have denoted humanistic ideas of spiritual freedom of the individual, although it appears to have been mostly directed to responsibility and hence punishability of man and, in addition, was quickly reinterpreted as 'autocracy'. It was so used by Ivan the Terrible, and in this sense it entered Russian literary language of the nineteenth century. Some iconoclastic tendencies that became visible are taken as evidence of nascent rationalist thought, as are the doubts that were cast on the concept of the Trinity.

The point, however, is not that all those ideas appeared in an inchoate and often confused form; and that they hardly can be described as an intellectual 'movement' in any meaningful sense, so that even a Soviet author has to admit that in dealing with 'Russian Reformation' one could speak only of a *povorot* [a turn in a certain direction] rather than of a *perevorot* [an upheaval].[22] The point rather is that all those matters are exquisitely irrelevant for the understanding of the Russian Schism. True, the two-finger cross and the double hallelujah were interpreted before and after the Schism as denoting the twofold nature of Christ, while the established Church regarded the three-finger cross and the treble hallelujah as symbolizing the Trinity. But since the Old Believers did not reject the Trinity—although some conversational controversies on the subject took place among the leaders of the early Old Believers[23]—and since the established Church did not reject the dual, that is, divine and human, nature of Christ, the divergence was devoid of substantive significance. In fact, the Old Believers regarded the three bent-in fingers as representing the Trinity and for the established Church the two bent-in fingers represented the dual nature of the Savior.

16

Try as one may, it is altogether impossible to discover in the intellectual history of the Russian Old Believers anything remotely reminiscent of, or in any way equivalent to, concepts such as predestination, unconditional election, or calling. The tenets of the bulk of the schismatics were also those of the established Church, including the worship of icons, the acceptance of the seven sacraments, and the belief that faith is made effective through observance of rites. It was only in the extreme branches of the Old Believers—the *bespopovtsy*, the priestless or non-sacerdotal ones—that the impossibility of ordainment led to the abandonment of the other sacraments (with the exception of baptism), usually leading to the adoption of analogous substitutions.[24]

Kliuchevskii made the point very clearly: 'The schismatics consider themselves orthodox Christians just as much as we do. The Old Believers in the proper sense of the word do not deviate from us in any single dogma of faith, in any fundamental tenet thereof.'[25] And in our time it was said by one of the most interesting and authoritative Orthodox authors: 'The Russian schism, if somewhat onesidedly, has preserved in its basic spiritual beliefs [*dukhovnyi uklad*] the spirit of the orthodox church.'[26]

Let me add in parentheses that later protestant sects of various persuasions did indeed constitute a challenge to the doctrines of the established Church, but those sects are of little interest in connection with the problem under discussion here.

Let me now turn to the economic consequences of the Schism, that is to say, the role played by the Old Believers in the economic history of the country, and more precisely in its economic development. The period to consider is the nineteenth century. The great spurt of Russian industrialization came in the last years of that century. In scrutinizing the forces that played the role

17

of strategic factors in that process no doubt the primary significance must be attributed to the policies of the Russian government and then to the importation of technological and commercial know-how, as well as of some entrepreneurial talent and capital from abroad. As will be shown later, it would be difficult to assign any significant part in this development to the Old Believers. But Russian economic development did not start with the great spurt, although the latter was very different both quantitatively and qualitatively from what had gone before it. And if we look at a number of decades preceding it, we find that the history of those years cannot be written without a great deal of emphasis on the contribution to Russian entrepreneurship made by Old Believers.

It is essentially in two geographic areas that the significant economic activities of the Old Believers were carried out: Moscow and its environs and the lands along both banks of the River Volga. There are no comprehensive studies of the Old Believers as entrepreneurs in trade or industry, and the evidence must be gleaned precariously and incompletely from a number of memoirs, a few general books, some ethnographic descriptions, including some celebrated ethnographic novels, and some government reports. No extensive biographies are available. The Soviet historians on the whole studiously avoid references to Old Believers as entrepreneurs. Peter Lyashchenko, for instance, devotes a number of pages in his *Economic History* to Moscow entrepreneurs and mentions a number of Old Believers among them by name, without ever pointing out their religious affiliation.[27] To do so seems to be, or at least to have been, taboo in relevant historical writings. Yet the general picture does emerge with sufficient clarity. It appears that there was a large number of Old Believers who achieved very considerable success as entrepreneurs, accumulated fortunes measured in millions of rubles, and founded what has come to be called 'merchant dynasties'. As early as the beginning of the eighteenth century, the Old Believers' community on the River Vyg in the north achieved considerable economic importance as a center of crafts and trade. In particular they were engaged in large-scale grain trade and became important in supplying grain to the young city of St Petersburg. They did so by utilizing their connections with other Old Believers' communities in the southern parts of the country. As Miliukov put it, this was the first example of an Old Believers' broad association in trade and industry based on absolute mutual confidence and on severe moral discipline.[28]

The founders of the 'dynasties' were mostly men of humble peasant origin. It is not clear how many of them had been serfs of the estate owners [*pomeshchiki*] or came from the ranks of the State or Imperial peasantry. It is clear, however, that all three categories were well represented. It appears that in many cases they began in trade, and particularly grain trade, including flour trade. In the far-flung regions along the Volga flour mills and saw mills, first driven by water and then by steam, were established, resulting in the 'milling empires' in the hands of the Old Believers. Along with that their strong participation in the Volga shipping and in the fisheries on the lower Volga as well as in fish trade must be mentioned. It was in Moscow, however, and within a relatively short distance from Moscow—in the Russian 'mesopotamia' between the upper Volga and the Oka rivers—that the Old Believers, particularly the merchants of the second generation, began to establish textile factories, some of them producing woolens, but most of them being cotton mills. In several cases, calico printing, carried to Moscow from the cottage industry in the villages, was the first step, to be followed by construction of spinneries, and weaving sheds. A German, Ludwig Knoop (1821–94), was the little Bremen apprentice to commerce, who after a year in Manchester came to Russia (in 1839) in his English

19

re-incarnation as the representative (or rather the assistant to a representative) of Lancashire. The talented youngster, one of the great entrepreneurial figures of the century, began as an importer of yarn and cloth, but very soon undertook to supply complete equipment to Russian cotton spinneries and later to weaving sheds. In addition, he brought from Lancashire skilled labor, foremen, and engineers. Over his lifetime he managed to establish in this fashion some 120-odd factories—surely one of the most remarkable examples of a massive borrowing of foreign technology (which, incidentally, for a year or two still proceeded in the face of the British prohibition against export of machinery). But it seems that the first Russian textile mill organized by Knoop was for the son of the Old Believer Savva Morozov, the founder of the ramified family who came to occupy a dominant position in the Russian textile industry. Some of the branches of the family remained faithful to the Old Believers' creed, while others tended to move away from it. Even a couple of decades earlier it was an Old Believer (Rogozhin) who introduced the first Jacquard loom into Russia. Altogether, the significance of the Old Believers' contribution to the textile industry, until the great spurt, the most important industry of the country, cannot be doubted. While the period of mechanization dates from about 1840, the influx of the Old Believers into Moscow followed the war of 1812 when the rebuilding of the burned-down city offered great opportunities both in trade and in industry. An area less favored by the Old Believers was contracting for the government and the farming of the trade in spirits [*vodka*]. Yet, it was the latter field that produced one of the most colorful entrepreneurial figures of the time with an astonishingly wide range of subsequent activities. The reference is to V. A. Kokorev, who came from an Old Believer family in the extreme north and became founder of the first oil company in Baku, of the significant Volga-Kama Bank, of a large insurance company, to say nothing of his participation in railroad construction.[29]

A preliminary conclusion emerges from what has been said so far. The Old Belief was a religious movement, destitute of independent doctrinal content and utterly conservative in outlook, seeking spiritual haven in the usages and customs of a past that was becoming more and more remote. It is not for nothing that along with the name of Old Believers [*starovery*] there was also the name of 'Old Ritualists' [*staroobryadtsy*] attached to the adherents of the movement. And yet, it was the members of such a group who displayed impressive entrepreneurial talents and engaged with great success in entrepreneurial activities on a large scale and over a wide range. The worshippers of religious immobility, the fanatical enemies of ecclesiastic reforms, the irrational adherents to letter and gesture appear as energetic modernizers in their very rational economic pursuits. This appears paradoxical indeed, and something more must be said about their *mores* and conduct so as to characterize them as a social group. But in order to do so, something must be also said about the position of Old Believers within the body social of the country, and this perforce means their relationship to the State. For it can be said of the Old Believers that they were essentially formed and perpetuated—not indeed deliberately, but none the less very effectively—by the State, that is to say, by the policies of the government; which I believe is true whether attention focuses on the group as a whole or on its élite. This should cause no surprise, if one considers that so many things in Russian history, including the formation of social classes, cannot be understood except by reference to the demiurgic force of the State.

These problems will be discussed in the following lecture which it is hoped will lead to a reasonable conclusion with regard to the relationship between the historical phenomenon of the Russian Old Believers and the Weber thesis. Thereafter I shall touch briefly on a historical episode which, without being related to the Schism, appears to cast some additional light on the Weber hypothesis.

2

In interpreting the entrepreneurial rise of the Old Believers, one must turn to the history of the group since its condemnation by the Council in 1666–7. It is a dark and sorrowful story, the first part of which—some four decades—was marked by monstrous cruelties. Violence began almost at once. A fortress-like island monastery in the far north (Solovki) was stormed by government troops after a siege that lasted for seven years. As the government embarked upon the repressions in and around Moscow, the Old Believers began to flee away from the center in all directions of the compass: westward to the densely-wooded areas of Belorussia and northern Ukraine, beyond the boundaries of the State, southward to the frontier areas on the Don and Kuban rivers, northward toward the Arctic shores, and eastward into the steppes and forests beyond the River Volga. In the eighties, they took some part in a military mutiny in the capital and caused considerable fermentation among the Don cossacks.[1] By that time, the leaders of the Old Believers with the Priest Avvakum at their head had been burned at the stake after having been imprisoned for fifteen years.

From then on the ferocity of the persecutions continued unabated. The decree of 1685, issued by the Regent Sophia, sanctioned burning at the stake for those who preached Old Belief and refused to repent after thrice repeated torture. Those who repented were to be sent to monasteries, the unmarried among them 'forever', and the relapse into Old Belief was to be punished by death. Those who offered, whether knowingly or unknowingly, food and lodging to the schismatic preachers were threatened with fines, floggings, and exile attended by confiscation of property. What followed was an orgy of repression and martyrdom. In the northern regions, suicides by fire became rife, prompted by apocalyptic despair, religious fervor, or fear of authorities. At times unthreatened, at times at the approach of government troops, whole communities of Old Believers, men, women, and children, would lock themselves in their wooden chapels or hermitage monasteries [*skity*] and set them on fire, preferring the self-inflicted death.[2] On the other hand, the government proceeded all over the country to burn at the stake, to chop off heads, to cut out nostrils and tongues, to administer murderous floggings, to jail, and to exile.

It is at least a moot question whether in doing so the government simply acted as the executive arm of the Church, as was suggested by Kliuchevskii,[3] or whether even in those earlier years of the Schism the government understood that in fighting religious dissent it was also fighting discontent produced by its own policies with regard to the peasantry. At any rate, with the advent to power of Peter the Great (1689) misapprehensions of this sort were no longer possible. Even if one grants that in the beginning the Schism was mainly an ecclesiastic phenomenon, directed against the Church and opposing the State only because the former was supported by the latter, in Peter's reign the Schism quickly acquired a pronounced political complexion.

When the young Tsar returned from abroad (1698) to suppress with extreme ruthlessness the uprising of the traditional military corps, the *Strel'tsy*, and embarked upon the road of modernizing State and society and developing the economy, the protest against innovations in texts and rituals quite naturally merged with the protest against innovations in areas outside the sphere of religion and with the opposition to the exorbitant

24

costs of the reform that were borne by the mass of the population. The *old* rites quite naturally connected themselves in the popular mind with the deeply ingrained collective memory of the *old* freedom. In the matter of serfdom, the peasants could be nothing but 'old believers'.

The enforced Europeanization was offensive to age-old customs, which were more than merely colored by religious beliefs. Beards and the 'Russian' dress had been regarded as symbols of religious decorum. Man had been created in the image of the Lord, and who could imagine God the Father, or Christ and the Saints for that matter, without beards? But the Tsar had ordered urban beards to be shaved and peasant beards to be taxed; he had sought to replace the traditional *kaftan*—so very Russian despite its Mongolian origin both in etymology and fact —by the simple device of having the long garment forcibly cut to 'German' length. He identified himself with the official Church by placing it under the rule of the absolutist State: when the Partiarch Adrian died (1700), the Tsar refused to have a successor elected, and, after two decades (1721), in his *Dukhovnyi Reglament* [Ecclesiastical Ordinance] he abolished the Patriarchate as well as the Church Councils, establishing by an edict the Most Holy Governing Synod. Thereby the Tsar assumed the position of the supreme head of the Church, exercising his control through a Chief Procurator—'the Tsar's eye'—which office was created a year later, its holder becoming more and more powerful in the following historical periods, attaining cabinet status in the early nineteenth century.[4] Even the residual freedom granted to the Church in matters of dogmas and canons came to refer in practice to little more than the conduct of the service and the ministering to the needs of the faithful.[5] For Peter did not hesitate to legislate on questions pertaining to the sacrament of marriage.[6] The Church so reformed became in the eyes of the Old Believers the handmaiden of an iniquitous secular power. And it was

Peter who crowned his proliferation of taxes by finally introducing the *podushnaya podat'*—the soul tax—unconcerned with the fact that it was nothing short of blasphemy to tax the divine in man, that is, his soul.

The reforming Tsar, taxing and conscripting, oppressing and exploiting, became an object of violent popular hatred, and it was the Old Believers who supplied the ideology of the opposition. Peter began to be viewed as the Antichrist. The apocalyptic 'number of the beast'— six hundred, three score and six (Rev. xiv.18)—was discovered in the name of the Tsar, and it was then found, after some manipulations, in the name of the later emperors, just as the early Christians had found it in the name of Nero (the number value of Hebrew consonants in 'Neron Caesar' adding up to 666). The Tsar, the Old Believers preached, was a false one. He was actually a Jew from the tribe of Dan, it was said, thus reviving a medieval view of Antichrist that had been widespread from the shores of the eastern Mediterranean to those of the Atlantic. Apocalyptic fears were nothing new in Russia. The coming of Antichrist was expected in 1492, the end of the seventh millennium since the creation of the world in accordance with the old calendar. The Roman popes had been widely regarded as the precursors of Antichrist. In fact, in the last quarter of the sixteenth century the English merchants in Moscow produced a book which described the Pope not as a precursor, but as the very phenomenon, and the Jesuit Possevino wrote a memorandum to the Tsar to disprove the charge.[7] It was natural for the Old Believers to view Patriarch Nikon as the precursor of Antichrist, and the year of the fateful Council of 1666—again containing the sinister number, this time according to the new 'godless' Julian calendar —was then also interpreted as adumbrating the end of the world. Such beliefs no doubt played considerable part in motivating the self-immolations of the Old Believers. It would be a mistake, however, to view those

26

beliefs in the long run as the crucial ingredient of the Old Belief—'the theme and mystery of the Schism'.[8] It would be difficult indeed to explain even the orderly husbandry of the old believing peasants, let alone the economic activities, including the accumulation of capital by the old-believing merchants and factory owners, in the light of a belief in the imminent end of the world. In the nineteenth century, men such as the previously mentioned Morozovs when investing in their factories had to look far into the future. And it is no more than a curiosity that while every one of his brothers was establishing a successful factory, Elisey Morozov chose to become an expert on the doctrine of Antichrist.[9] What no doubt had fully and generally survived among the Old Believers into the nineteenth century was 'the deepest hatred' of Peter the Great, as Haxthausen discovered in his conversations with the schismatics.[10]

It is not surprising, therefore, that in the two large popular rebellions against Peter—in Astrakhan (1705–6) and on the River Don (the so-called Bulavin's rebellion, 1707–8, in which even some Old Believing monks are said to have participated as leaders—the economic demands of the rebels, their protest against State and serfdom, were inextricably commingled with the protest against the 'Greek faith' and the 'German dress' coupled with promises to fight for 'the house of the Holy Virgin and the true Christian faith.'[11] In fact, so much stress was laid on these points that modern Soviet historians still upbraid the leaders of the rebellions for their immaturity and backwardness in letting the economic and social aims of the movement be overshadowed by religious issues.[12]

The fierceness of the persecutions was considerably relaxed in the last nine years of Peter's reign. The Old Believers received the right to live openly in villages and towns provided that they registered as such and submitted themselves to a discriminating taxation ('double imposition'). There were many reasons why the Old

27

Believers' image of the Tsar did not change as a result of these alleviations. Many Old Believers, distrustful as they were of the government, hesitated to register; an inquisitorial procedure was instituted to discover the secret Old Believers who had failed to register and to deal with those who did register after having posed as members of the established Church; then the question would arise whether they had recently joined the Schism, and attempts to convert outsiders to Old Belief were still punishable by forced labor; the Old Believers remained excluded from elective offices in the villages and towns and prohibited from testifying at courts against Christians belonging to the established Church; and, finally, they were forced to wear a special strictly-prescribed dress with distinctive marks in conspicuous colors, including, for the women, hats with horns upon them.

After Peter's reign, the policy fluctuated. The repressive measures were intensified between the thirties and the sixties. The short reign of Peter III and then that of Catherine II brought some liberalizations. Old Believers who had fled to Poland were allowed to return and settled along an eastern tributary of the Volga (Irgiz). The fatal disability of being barred from bearing witness at courts was abolished in 1769. In 1782, the requirement of double taxation was rescinded and so were the repressive measures, largely directed against the Old Believers' chapels, praying houses, and monasteries [*skity*]. Still, when the Pugachev uprising broke out in 1773, a rebellion that threatened the empire with extreme peril and is not incorrectly described by Soviet historians as the Russian Peasant War, the leader of the uprising was quite conscious of the Old Believers and their discontent. This was natural. Pugachev was a Don cossack who had participated in the Russian campaigns against Prussia and Turkey and then got himself into trouble with the authorities. While a fugitive, he received aid and support from the Old Believers in different parts of the country until, posing as an Old Believer allegedly returning from Poland, he was sent to the Irgiz. It was among the Old Believers that he heard about the great unrest among the Ural cossacks and apparently in conversations with Old Believers conceived the idea of impersonating the late Emperor, Peter III. At any rate, in the course of the uprising, in his imperial manifestoes addressed to the 'whole Russian people', Pugachev promised not only emancipation from serfdom, that is 'freedom and liberty' [*svobodu i voliu*—words taken from Peter III's manifesto in 1762 regarding the emancipation of the gentry]; not only abolition of conscription and of all taxes, as well as 'full ownership of fields and forests, meadows and fisheries . . . without payment of purchase or quitrent'; but also 'the old cross, and prayer, and beard'—the social, economic, and religious protests thus again merging quite naturally in one long sentence.[13]

It was, however, during the same reign that in the 1780s the first attempts were made to facilitate the return of the Old Believers to the established Church by creating the category of 'Like-Believers' [*Edinovertsy*]. They were allowed to retain their rites and their texts at the price of submitting themselves to the hierarchy of the established Church and of accepting its clergy. Under Catherine's successor, Paul I, these arrangements, first applied to vulnerable border areas, were then (1800) generalized for the whole territory.

Under Nicholas I (1825–55) and actually in the last years of his predecessor Alexander I, the trend was reversed and the restrictions were again intensified. Bars on bearing testimony in civil suits were reintroduced. Access to secondary schools and universities was allowed only at the price of joining the established Church. The gentry were instructed not to tolerate Old Believers as aldermen in their villages. After 1848, when a period of stiff reaction began in Russia in response to the revolutions in west and central Europe, a wholesale attack on

Old Believers' chapels and monasteries was initiated and special taxation in favor of the established Church imposed. In 1853, even farther-reaching programs were conceived to be implemented by a special secret committee. But the Crimean War and the death of the Emperor prevented the execution of those plans. With the period of liberal reforms under Alexander II, began a gradual abolition of discrimination. But it was not until the years of general unrest preceding the 1905 revolution that a wide measure of tolerance in religious matters was finally proclaimed (the edict of April 17/30 1905), and an end was put to two and a half centuries of persecution.[14]

What then did the government policies in their varying severity accomplish? They failed in their object of leading the Old Believers back to the fold of the Church. But they may have unwittingly compounded the failure and produced results that were the very opposite of their goals. The simple failure, of course, was obvious. The numbers of Old Believers must be presumed to have grown very much faster than the rate of growth of the population.[15] The Old Believers remained faithful to the old prayer, the two-finger cross, and the double allelujah. Was this astonishing? The fanatical adherence of the Old Believers to formal rites and to the letter of the text must not be dismissed with a contemptuous smile. If simple—and sometimes not so simple—minds are to take religious verities as absolute truths, never to be doubted, the words in which they are couched must be covered with the patina of ages and the rituals must be sanctified by a long tradition. At the end of the eighteenth century it was not an Old Believer but Admiral Shishkov, a statesman and a loyal follower of the established Church, who objected to the change from the traditional Church-Slavonic version of the Scripture to a Russian one by asking: 'How can one dare to change words that are considered to have issued from divine lips?'[16] It should be remembered in particular that in Russia the sign of the cross was not just something that was confined to service in churches. It pervaded the whole life of the Russian. It was made on joyous and triste, grave and trite occasions. The peasant crossed himself before he urged his wooden plow upon a new furrow. The mother crossed the child when tucking him in for the night. A yawning mouth was crossed to protect the body from evil spirits. What is astonishing rather was the ability of the established Church to introduce changes of this kind, and it took a long time to do so. Even in the sixties of the nineteenth century, there were whole provinces where about one-third of the members of the established Church continued to use the two-finger cross.[17]

Nevertheless, this cannot be the whole story. It is quite unlikely that the Schism would have become a mass movement without the policy of the absolutist State which enserfed and enslaved, taxed and conscripted. Without Peter's reforms adherents of Old Belief hardly would have grown to be numbered in millions. But even this supposition cannot be divorced from the specific policies of the government against the Old Believers and the variations in the intensity of the repressions.

Two centuries of persecution and discrimination, far from breaking the resistance of the Old Believers, must be considered as decisive in forming both the sociological complexion of the group and the achievements of the individuals that belonged to it. The crucial point is the measure of intolerance to which they were subject. Had the violent and cruel repressions of the early decades after the Schism continued unabated, the result would have been a small group of fanatics, completely isolated from the rest of the society. Complete tolerance might have produced a large group which distinguished itself from the rest of the population by the few deviations in rituals, but otherwise would have been well assimilated to the ways of living and acting that pervaded the mass of the population. But the tolerance would have to have been practiced from the very beginning. When the government finally bethought itself to create the category of 'Like-Believers' (see above), it was too late. The conversions to Like-Belief were relatively small and often very fictitious. Besides, the position of the Church remained ambiguous and for long decades the nice question continued to be debated as to whether the establishment of Like-Belief meant abrogation of the anathemas that had been pronounced in 1667 against the rituals of the Old Believers. But even a more open-minded attitude would have been of little avail. By the beginning of the nineteenth century the unity and the cohesiveness of the Old Belief in its main branches had been firmly established by the whole preceding history of intolerance. That intolerance, however, was of a special kind. In the long run, despite all the fluctuations in government policies, the intolerance must be described as persistent but not extreme; and even in periods of renewed severe persecutions, the intensity of intolerance was held in check by the easy corruptibility of the civil service. And the corruptibility of the civil service itself could not have been truly effective without the parallel accumulation of wealth and economic power on the part of some members of the group.

It was during the more liberal period under Catherine II that the Old Believers were able to form considerable organizations—cemeteries or 'ententes' they were called—which greatly increased the strength of the group, or rather groups. For, as said before, within the Old Belief there was the split between the so-called *popovtsy* —the 'priestly' group, to which the majority of the Old Believers adhered—and the *bespopovtsy*—the priestless group. The organization was of particular importance to the 'priestly' group. For no one—they believed—could function as a priest unless properly ordained by a bishop. While they rejected the 'Greek' Church, they still accepted its sole power to ordain. This meant either using 'fugitive priests' who could be induced to leave the official Church and allow themselves to be 're-anointed', as was required of 'heretics of the second class'; or alternatively, to secure an ecumenically ordained bishop who in turn could ordain the priests. The dearth of priests came to constitute a serious problem, and particularly so as a result of the repressive policies pursued by Nicholas I. One solution was to establish an episcopal see beyond the frontiers of Russia in the neighboring Bukovina (which had become Austrian in 1775) and have the priests ordained there. After long efforts a bishop was found and installed in 1846. Old Believers' communities had started in Bukovina as early as 1783 under the protection of Joseph II's Tolerance Patent (1781). The maintenance of the colony abroad was a costly operation and would have been impossible without the existence of the *Rogozhskoye* cemetery or 'entente' in Moscow; which again would have been little effective without the Moscow merchants and industrialists who had acquired positions of leadership within the organization.

The establishment of the 'ententes' and their concentration in Moscow was certainly a crucial landmark in the history of the Schism. As Simmel once remarked, a weak minority must seek dispersal; a strong minority must seek concentration.[18] He might have added that under favorable circumstances the change from dispersal to concentration can be a condition for increasing the strength of the minority. When after long years of dispersal in far away forests and steppes some Old Believers came out into the open, they did make themselves more vulnerable to potential persecution, but on balance the net gain in strength was obvious.

At the same time, intolerance breeds intolerance. To be sure, there was no longer the aggressive intolerance of the first decades when Avvakum wistfully spoke of the very dear and good Tsar Ivan the Terrible who without much ado simply would have strung up Avvakum's adversaries like mad dogs[19] (which is not unsimilar in our times to Sholokhov's regretful reference to the good old times when the writers guilty of opposing the Soviet regime would have received a swifter and more radical punishment than merely years of servitude in labor camps). The Old Believers were on the defensive. But they sought to isolate themselves in daily life as much as possible from those who did not see the light of the true Church. Accordingly, no Old Believer would enter an official church. They would not use dishes—bowls, and cups, and spoons—from which the rest of the population ate or drank. They abhorred the devilish habit of smoking tobacco. They objected to the Western innovations of coffee and potatoes, and it took them a long time to accept the tea which came from the Orient. And even though economic interest was sufficiently strong to overcome their antagonism to cotton, a leading Old Believer, a great entrepreneur, who had remained aloof from the textile industry, once upbraided his brethren for abandoning the native flax and wool in favor of an alien exotic fibre.[20] The Old Believers tried as best they could not to use the modern Julian calendar which was introduced by Peter the Great and to retain a calendar which counted the years from the creation of the world. In general, it can be said that it is matters pertaining to daily routine that contribute so strongly to the inner strength of the group, the absence of a *commensium* being perhaps even more important than that of a *connubium*, creating as it does a clear boundary line in everyday life.

In its defensive reaction against intolerance, the group builds up a feeling of moral superiority to the outsider and then proceeds to bolster that feeling by developing habits that both evidence and vindicate it. Hence came the features of cleanliness, honesty, reliability, frugality, industry and thrift that were so generally observed to characterize the Old Believers. In the same connection must be mentioned the greater literacy of the group. This is paradoxical, because in a sense ignorance and illiteracy of the Old Believers is usually seen as having lain at the basis of the Schism. The interest in the old texts, the dearth of priests among the *popovtsy* and their absence among the *bespopovtsy*, the frequent compulsion to withdraw to the secrecy of private praying chambers—all these contributed to the spread of literacy, even though along with it went the rejection of worldly literature. In some limited sense, a Russian historian was right when he described the Old Belief as an instrument of popular education,[21] a significant phenomenon in a country where schools for the peasantry were viewed with suspicion because literacy was seen as leading to restiveness and disobedience to authorities. It is perhaps also noteworthy in this connection that the Old Believers developed their own ciphered language, both spoken and written, based on an interchange of consonants, and added to the cipher a special lexical code. A secret language, of course, is nothing unusual as a defense instrument of a persecuted group.

Finally, there is the attitude toward money making and accumulation of wealth with respect to which, too, the Old Believers were in a position different from the rest of the population. The prevailing value system among the latter was hostile to the acquisition of wealth. The true God pleasing activity was tilling the soil, which was God's, and the orthodox merchant was driven to give money to his church in order to appease his guilty conscience. By contrast, for the Old Believer acquisition of money was necessary in order to support the continuing functioning of his church. Without money it was impossible to buy the priests, to maintain the Austrian establishment at Fontana Alba (Belaya Krinitsa), to support the numerous *skity*, to pay the representatives of the State, beginning from the powerful inspectors sent out from St Petersburg and the high and mighty governors of provinces all the way down to petty police officers, in order to induce them to look the other way and to tolerate activities that were proscribed by the law. Under these circumstances, it would be natural for members of a group, which after all was deeply religious, however formalistic its religion, to regard economic activities which were essential to the preservation of the group as highly pleasing to the Lord. It is not argued, of course, that nothing except his devotion determined the actions of the Old Believing entrepreneur. The fact that the entrepreneurial activities actually yielded wealth far in excess of what was needed, or at least used, for the defense of the group, and that fortunes of many millions were accumulated, should indicate the complexity of the relations between motivation and vindication. But it can be argued that vindication was not just a light veneer spread over crudely materialistic interests and aspirations.

Besides, the existence of organized groups of Old Believers had a twofold economic significance. On the one hand, there were the *faux frais* of graft payments and charitable activities. But on the other hand, there were the common bonds which meant mutual aid when credit was needed; meant also the possibility of raising on all levels a stock of trustworthy co-religious helpers in business activities whom very often the entrepreneur provided with the funds needed to buy freedom from serf-status. At the same time, it should be noted that there is considerable evidence to suggest that at least some of the positive qualities of the old-believing entrepreneur underwent modification in dealing with the members of the outside group. In particular when it came to dealing with masses of manual labor—say the *burlaki* [the barge haulers on the Volga]—fear of the Lord did not seem to prevent ruthless exploitation and crude deceit. And they were ever ready to quote the warning from the book of Jesus, the son of Sirach (not regarded as apocryphal by the Russian Church and considered deutero-canonical by the Catholic Church), against showing kindness to the unrighteous and the ungodly: 'Give to the righteous and give not to the sinner', says the Russian translation (12.1-4).[22]

Thus the old-believing entrepreneur on the whole did reveal traits which Max Weber was willing to regard as the specific capitalist spirit. There is no doubt that his economic activities appeared to him as guided, however loosely, by an ethically colored maxim. But the fount and origin of this value system cannot be found in his religious tenets. It stems with great clarity from the specific social position of the group of which he was a member. In fact, the religious teachings were contrary to the motivations which kept transforming Old Believing serf peasants into successful entrepreneurs. Avvakum, whose words were holy to the ears of the Old Believers, had said 'Whoever has been called to whatsoever shall remain therein'.[23] This was rightly interpreted as signifying the indifference of the Old Believers' creed to advancement on the social ladder. Thus the very idea of 'calling' to the minor extent that it was present had a meaning entirely different from what Weber has attributed to Calvinism. It made for stagnation rather than for change.

An interesting general idea may be referred to in this connection. Professor Everett Hagen in his highly stimulating and equally controversial book *On the Theory of Social Change* has attempted, even though cursorily, to bring the Old Believers under the wings of his theoretical construction.[24] In his view the general pattern leading to the rise of modern entrepreneurship is as follows: at a certain point in the history of the 'traditional society' respect is withdrawn from a certain low stratum by a powerful group. What follows is a long period of 'retreatism' in the course of which fundamental changes take place within the lap of the family. The position of the father who has lost his social status is gravely shaken; by the same token that of the mother is enhanced. This transforms the process of child rearing. The child no longer oppressed by the powerful father is treated in a fashion which reduces his aggressive urges and redirects them towards 'creativity'; the eventual result of this change in personality formation is the emergence within the society of a considerable group of creative men who are willing and able to act as innovators. Then growth can begin.

I have criticized this theory as unhistorical and non-operational.[25] But since, as I have said, Professor Hagen uses the Russian Old Believers as one of his examples, it should be in order to do both: to point out the extent to which the history of the Old Believers bears out my criticism; and at the same time to concede that the same history offers some traces of limited evidence in support of Professor Hagen's view.

There is a body of evidence, perhaps not overwhelming but quite considerable, concerning the family life of Old Believers. A deeply conservative group, wedded to the Russian value system of the pre-Petrine period, they observed within the family the tradition laid down by the sets of instructions composed and published in the first half of the sixteenth century. I am referring to the so-called *Domostroy*—the House Management, a literal translation of the Greek *oikonomia*—which in particular stressed the dominant position of the father within the family and, among other things, explained in which way and to which parts of the anatomy of wives and children corporal punishment by the father should be administered, the retribution varying with the gravity of the offense. True, the *Domostroy* was not a description of the barbarous reality of Russian family life, except indirectly by what it criticized. As was stressed by Kizevetter (among others), the *Domostroy* was a didactic pamphlet. It taught moderation. Wooden and iron implements, it advised, should not be employed in beating wives (though not children), such use having often led to blindness and deafness and likely to have caused abortions. By contrast, the positive qualities of the whip were highly praised, its application described as being 'reasonable and painful, frightening and healthy'. Still, the instructions of the *Domostroy* were a rather drastic elaboration of St Paul's admonition to wives to submit to their husbands (Col. 3.18), and the father was firmly called upon to 'inflict wounds' on disobedient sons, and in the process to use a more effective instrument than the whip.[26]

Much of what we know about the regimen in Old Believers' homes breathes the same spirit. Children and wives living in fear and trepidation of the father is indeed the usual picture of the Old Believers' family life in which the *patria potestas* seemed quite unlimited. Lashing wives and children with the *lestovka*, the previously mentioned leather rosary, was the mildest form of punishment, the more substantial whip being an essential tool in maintaining fatherly authority. In fact, an old wedding custom in Russia required the father of the bride to hand over a whip to the bridegroom as a token of his authority over the wife.[27] And the Old Believers, conservative and tradition-bound as they were, fully accepted the custom, and the whip never remained a mere token. The Old Believers liked to repeat the admonition of the ever-quotable Jesus, the son of Sirach: 'Press down the neck of thy son in his youth and crush his ribs as long as he is young, lest he become stubborn and disobedient to thee' (30.12).[28] The father may have been 'retreatist' within the society at large, but this did not seem to prevent him from fully acting the part of an autocrat and often that of a tyrant within the family.[29]

And yet, this in not the complete story. There are indications that at least in some branches of the Schism the position of the woman was changed and enhanced. There are, standing at the threshold of the Schism, the impressive figures of the two sisters—Morozova and Urusova; the two noblewomen were tortured and then died as martyrs for their faith, being starved to death in jail, and have been venerated as saints by the Old Believers. There is, moreover, the testimony of Avvakum himself whose father was a drunkard and whose praying and fasting mother taught him the fear of the Lord. When Avvakum hesitated before attacking what he called 'the heretical winter abroad', it was his wife who encouraged him to fight for the true faith.[30] It is a moot question whether these early examples did or did not affect later attitudes.

More important, however, are the statements concerning the 'Schism's raising the women to the dignity of preceptors on a basis of equality with men.'[31] The quotation is from A. P. Shchapov who was perhaps the first scholar to deal with the social and political basis of the Russian Schism.[32] There are a few remarks of that sort. spread over his writings on the subject, but they are made cursorily, and one looks in vain for elaboration and evidence.[33] Moreover, it seems clear that they essentially refer not to the totality of the Old Believers, but to the 'priestless' branch in the far north and mostly to the more radical sections of that group. It is perhaps noteworthy that even with regard to these sections, Shchapov admits the continuing influence of the *Domostroy*.[34] It should perhaps also be noted in this connection that the Old Believers had a very high female : male ratio in the population. The Old Believers' ratio according to the 1897 Census was 114.24:100, whereas the ratio of the Orthodox population was 102.83:100.[35]

Taking it in all for all, there is evidence that in the far north, on the shores of the White Sea, the position of woman in the family had changed not inconsiderably, and it is possible that the Schism was partly responsible for the change. But there were also other and less deeply-lying reasons. The men in the far north were engaged in high sea fishing during the short summer seasons, and trekked south in search of labor for the rest of the year.

At times, they came down as far as the Ukraine. In the 1840s the large stone bridge over the River Dnieper in Kiev, the so-called chain bridge, was built largely by a labor force composed of northern Old Believers. It was, it is claimed, the prolonged absence of the father from the family hearth that accounted for the greater independence of the women who found themselves mainly responsible for the task of raising the children.[36] Indeed in the entrepreneurial history of the Old Believers there is one case where the strong guiding influence of the mother is explicitly mentioned. This is the previously-mentioned case of Kokorev, surely an outstanding figure as an entrepreneur.[37] One case does not support a general theory and the far north was much less important in supplying entrepreneurs than the less remote regions. And in these regions, as said before, the *Domostroy* tradition continued unshaken. Still this grain of truth in the form of such empirical evidence as may be contained in Professor Hagen's theory in its application to the Old Believers should not have gone unmentioned.

It is another matter that as far as withdrawal of respect from a group is concerned, the enserfment of the masses of the Russian peasantry, that is to say, their virtual transformation into slaves to the *pomeshchik*, was a much more drastic manifestation of the phenomenon. There, no change in the position of the women and in the treatment of children was ever noticed. And it is still another matter that supply of the entrepreneurs is only one and perhaps not the most important condition of industrialization. In saying that I have in mind among other things, the crucial transformation in entrepreneurial behavior, in the standards of honesty, and in the attitude toward time horizon, that occurs in the very process of industrialization.[38]

And this leads to the final points that must be made here. The fact of the Old Believers' participation in the creation of modern textile industry in Russia cannot be

41

doubted. At the same time, the historical significance of that participation must not be exaggerated. After all, along with the Old Believers there were large numbers of textile industrialists who were members of the established Church. It is perhaps only with regard to the economic activities beyond the River Volga that one could speak of the prevalence of the Old Believers, particularly in the milling industry. And still more important is something else, to which reference has been made before. The early development of the textile industry, even though large enough to enrich the owners concerned, was, prior to the abolition of serfdom, greatly handicapped by the competition of gentry factories and the cottage industry of the peasants. It could not give rise to a great spurt of Russian industrialization. The great spurt required the assistance and guidance by the State, and it also required changing the emphasis in the development of industry from consumers' goods to producers' goods. It required the use of the most modern technology, and one of the charges that after some time had begun to be leveled against Knoop was that when importing factories from England, he was too frequently satisfied with the purchase of somewhat dated technology. In short, when the hour of real industrialization in the country struck, it would be in vain to look for practicing Old Believers as entrepreneurs making any notable contribution to the spurt. New men came, unbound by tradition, maintaining close commercial and intellectual contacts with the West, and eager to work together with the government authorities.

The suspicion of, if not disloyalty against, the State was deeply rooted in the Old Believers' philosophy. Historians often raised the question as to what would have been the outcome of Napoleon's invasion in Russia, if he had decided to proclaim the emancipation of the serfs. Similarly, from time to time the counter-factual question was raised as to what would have happened if Napoleon had ordered an Old Believers' service to be held, after an appropriate re-consecration, in the Cathedral of the Assumption in the Kremlin. It might be noted that, as Haxthausen discovered at least among one of the Russian sects, there was a tendency to view Napoleon as 'the lion in the valley of Jehosaphat who was destined to overthrow the false emperor and restore the throne to the White Tsar.'[39] The Old Believers' center in Austria caused considerable apprehension to the Russian government, because of the way in which it might be used by the Austrian government in the case of a military conflict. And above all, the collective memories of the brutal persecutions by the government continued to stand between the Old Believers and the State.

The great spurt of Russian industrialization had to do without the Old Believers, and, in fact, without any specifically ethically-colored maxims whether stemming from religious doctrines or from the specific situation of a persecuted group. There is no evidence that the experience accumulated in the earlier years benefited the entrepreneurs of the later days. The Russian historian Kostomarov suggested that, in the earlier period, the Old Believing entrepreneurs were more literate than the entrepreneurs belonging to the established Church, and he was willing to attribute to that circumstance the Old Believers' greater economic success.[40] But the Russian entrepreneurs of the 1890s possessed a modern European education and were in this respect, as in many others, incomparably superior to their Old Believing predecessors of the 1840s and of the following decades. The successors were different men in thought and action. If the spirit that pervaded them was the same capitalist spirit, it had little to do with the value system of the Old Believers. Gone was the distrust of the State and the abhorrence of 'German' customs. A gulf seems to separate the two. If some role can be assigned to the Old Believers in the great spurt and thereafter it is not in the entrepreneurial

43

sector. The only thing that may be noted was the preference of entrepreneurs and managers for the Old Believer as industrial laborer, primarily because of his temperance which was a factor of considerable importance in a country where consumption of alcohol greatly influenced the rate of absenteeism and beyond it the general reliability of industrial workers. The distinction between *piushchie* and *nepiushchie*, between drinking and non-drinking men, was paramount in the minds of those who hired workers and foremen.

Still, the story of the Old Believers does shed some, at least indirect, light on the plausibility of Max Weber's hypothesis. In discussing the sociological significance of rituals, Max Weber used to point out that they were directly opposed to the tenets of puritanism in that their observance deflected man from the pursuits of gainful employment.[41] But here was a group of people who not only took over with greatest scrupulousness the extensive ritual of the Greek Orthodox Church, but whose divergence and deviation from that Church exhausted itself in minutiae which altogether pertained to the sphere of rituals. Furthermore, Weber placed much emphasis on the rationalist elements in protestantism, and those going beyond Weber could argue that protestant views merged readily with the impact of enlightenment. There was nothing in the doctrines of the Old Believers, as indeed in those of the Greek Orthodox Church, that pointed in that direction. Mysticism rather than rationalism was the dominant feature of the faith. And yet, the cotton mills of Old Believing entrepreneurs, within the abilities of the men, were rationally conducted enterprises and as such emanations of 'rational bourgeois capitalism' in which, as Talcott Parsons insists, Max Weber was principally interested.[42]

Moreover, one must not forget that it was the established Church that was carrying out a reform of sorts. Unlike the protestant Reformation, the Russian Church did not touch on fundamental dogmas, but it did attempt to correct the errors and distortions of the holy texts. It was not much of a Reformation. It has been argued that the actual Russian Reformation was carried out not by the Church but by the police State of Peter the Great. 'Peter's Ecclesiastic Ordinance is the program of Russian Reformation',[43] and the Church is said to have protested against its secularization, the importation of the foreign heresy, 'in stormy whispers'.[44] The subjugated Church, whose clergy was not exempt from corporal punishment until the edicts of Catherine II in the 1760s and 1770s, had indeed much reason to protest. But to whatever degree what had happened in Church or State was comparable to the Reformation in the West, the Old Believers were bitterly opposed to it and their protest was a great deal louder than whispers, however 'stormy'. If Church and State were engaged in a Reformation, the Old Believers' movement was clearly counter-reformatory.

Finally, it must be said that not even the much attenuated version of Max Weber's theory could be said to have held in Russia. If in the West protestant faith was espoused because its world view was more consonant with men's new worldly preoccupations, no one in Russia *became* an Old Believer for this reason. If peasants or workers, employed by the Old Believers in cottage industry or in the factories, allowed themselves to be converted to their masters' faith, this was done for economic and social rather than for ideological reasons.

The conclusion, therefore, that emerges with some force from this little exercise in comparative history is as follows: since the Old Believers did not leave the established Church for any doctrinal divergences, they constitute a rather uniquely suitable case for testing a crucial element in Max Weber's hypothesis. Their case appears to show that the social condition of a penalized, persecuted group affords sufficient impulse for the members of such a group to engage in profitable economic activities and to develop traits that Max Weber considered as specific appurtenances of the 'capitalist spirit'. By the same token some doubt is cast on the significance of Calvinist doctrines for the rise of modern capitalism.

This should not be a surprising conclusion. This is what Sir William Petty had asserted nearly 270 years ago when he said 'that trade is not fixed to any species of religion as such, but rather . . . to the heterodox part of the whole.'[45] It is interesting to note that Max Weber, while several times referring to, and quoting from, Petty's 'Political Arithmetic' avoids quoting the crucial conclusion of 'so able an observer'.[46]

It was Petty's conclusion at which Werner Sombart finally arrived in his *Modern Capitalism*, except that, burdened as he was with the dead weight of his previous excursions into the doctrines of Judaism, he had to qualify his statement by agreeing that 'certain doctrines tended to solidify [*versteifen*] the capitalist spirit', even though, he added, there were also many obstacles to the development of that spirit contained precisely in the teachings of the puritans and the quakers.[47]

When Schulze-Gaevernitz in the early 1890s studied the economy of Russia, the historical connection between the economic activities of the Old Believers and their minority position within Russia's body social could not escape his sharp eye. He had no difficulty in explaining what he saw in terms of Petty's generalization, to whom he expressly referred.[48] It should be noted that Schulze-Gaevernitz did his research and published his findings years before the appearance of Max Weber's essay. Had the time sequence been reversed, it is very likely indeed that, armed with his knowledge of the Old Believers' experience, Schulze-Gaevernitz would have held Petty against Max Weber, as I have tried to do in the preceding pages.

As a result of their specific position, the Old Believers may be said then to have made their contribution to

Russian capitalism and the emergence of the capitalist spirit in the country. But both capitalism and the spirit thereof are vague terms which defy measurement. They are of little help to an economic historian unless they can be related to quantitative aspects of economic development in general and of industrial development in particular. And in these terms it is quite meaningful to say that the hour of Russian capitalism did not strike until the last years of the nineteenth century. The previously-mentioned fact that the Old Believers' contribution to that crucial phase of the development was minimal reveals the limitations that exist upon what can be achieved by a penalized minority and tends to lend support to Schumpeter's basic view that entrepreneurs are likely to spring forth from all layers and segments of society.

At the same time, the clear lack of spiritual continuity between entrepreneurs that came from the ranks of the Old Believers and the entrepreneurs of the last years of the past century appears to me to be an interesting aspect of the broad proposition, to wit, that the industrial development in a backward country is characterized by more pronounced discontinuity than that of more advanced countries. The comparison of the degree of such discontinuities with regard to matters such as changes in the rate of industrial growth or the modes of financing industrial development do help us understand not only the course of economic history in the backward country, but also the nature of that history in the more advanced countries. And it is interesting to note that in this respect also the entrepreneurial history of the Old Believers is an integral part of the general problem of Russia versus Europe.

Quite independent of the conclusions with regard to the Old Believers, there is a curious episode in Russian history which occurred in the seventeenth century and thus coincides in time with the origins of the Russian

Schism, but is unconnected with it. This episode, concrete and minor as it is, does again have some bearing on an important aspect of Max Weber's hypothesis. I am referring to the strange life of Yurii Krizhanich, a non-Russian who became an important figure in Russian intellectual history of that century.

Krizhanich—or Juraj Križanić according to the Croation spelling—was born in a little town in Croatia, near Zagreb, probably in 1618, the fateful year which was marked by the outbreak of the Thirty Years' War. A devout catholic, he went first to the Seminary at Zagreb and then continued his studies in the capital of Styria, Graz, close to the very focus of the Counter-Reformation in central Europe.[49] After having obtained his master's degree in Graz, he finished his formal theological education in Bologna, and was ordained in Rome in 1640. Thereupon, he was accepted by the Collegium Sancti Athanasii in order to prepare there for work among Greek Orthodox Christians in Croatia with a view to converting them to catholicism (1641). But the young man was already possessed by conversion plans, much more grandiose in nature. For in the same year 1641, he submitted a remarkable memorandum to Antonio Barberini, the prefect general of the Sacra Congregatio de Propaganda Fide at the Curia Romana. This memorandum contained a most ambitious program and decisively shaped Krizhanich's life. The purpose was to terminate the schism of the Churches by leading Russia back to the fold of the Catholic Church. This was a difficult but entirely feasible enterprise. For Russia, Krizhanich argued, was not truly heretical. It merely had been seduced by the Byzantines owing to Russian backwardness and ignorance. And Krizhanich proposed himself as the instrument chosen to bring about the conversion. The practical procedure, the strategy to be followed was set forth in some detail in Part III of the memorandum. Krizhanich was to go to Russia and to find access to the Tsar. In the process great circumspection was necessary, he explained. For the Tatar domination had made the Russians *astuti e dolosi* [crafty and cunning], and extremely suspicious of other nations. It would be necessary first to win their trust by making oneself useful to throne and country as a source of important knowledge in theoretical and practical matters pertaining to religion, war and peace, and general education, including mathematics and the reform of the calendar. The period of *circuizioni ed ambagi* [of circumventions and circumlocutions] might take four or five or even more years, but eventually confidence would be won, and then the first step would be to explain to the Tsar that his great historical mission consisted in breaking the grip of the Turks over Europe and in liberating the Christians smarting under the yoke of the infidels. But after the mind of the Tsar had been ignited by the sense of the high task, in the service of Christendom, he would be told that its successful implementation required the aid of the catholic nations, because the Tsar's own military might and military know-how were insufficient for the purpose: and, finally, that the catholic powers could not be prevailed upon to help and to make common cause with the Tsar, unless the ancient schism could be removed by Russia's abandoning the Greek heresy and joining the Roman Catholic Church.[50]

The plan may have interested the Congregation whose purpose after all was directed *in partes infidelium*. In the preceding century, the successes of the Reformation made Rome very eager to offset the losses in the West by extending its influence in the East. In 1580, a Jesuit, Antonio Possevino, was sent to Moscow in order to explore the possibilities of a union. It was Possevino's report on his travels which Krizhanich had read and quoted at length in his memorandum and which must have largely inspired him. But for the time being, Krizhanich was given a parish in Croatia and then in Slavonia, where he spent busy years preparing himself for the great mission.

49

In 1646, he was sent as a priest to Smolensk, which was (since 1634) again Polish. On the way there, always mindful of increasing his future usefulness in Russia, he acquired in Vienna a volume dealing with the ways and means of increasing the revenues of State treasuries.[51] In the following year he managed, stubbornly overcoming many obstacles, to join a Polish embassy to Moscow and spent several weeks there (October–December 1647), whereupon, after some more delays and travels, he returned to Rome to report on his experience and to urge permission to go to Russia for an extended stay there. It seems that permission was withheld, or rather was given by the Congregation but not approved of by the Pope. At any rate, Krizhanich, apparently alleging that he was still covered by the old permission of 1646, proceeded in 1658 to Moscow.

He arrived there in September of 1659, and for some time things seemed to be proceeding most satisfactorily. Krizhanich established connections with two of the highest and very influential dignitaries of the Court, I. M. Rtishchev and B. N. Morozov (the latter was the Tsar's brother-in-law). Both men were greatly interested in Western secular culture, but also in the Latin erudition of the Kievan monks.[52] Krizhanich was given a salary and, with the approval of his high protectors, undertook to write a refutation of the travelogue by Olearius which was published first in 1647 and in which many things Russian appeared in a very unfavorable light.[53] Things could not have been better, but the auspicious beginning proved deceptive. The great plan went awry, and in January 1661, hardly sixteen months after his arrival, Krizhanich found himself a-traveling again, still in the easterly direction, on his way into a Siberian exile at Tobolsk.

The reasons for the banishment are not clear. Many years later, Krizhanich himself gave a very unconvincing reason for the deportation, but also referred to a 'foolish word' he had uttered in a conversation.[54] It has been suggested that meddling with Russia's Swedish and Polish affairs, or some criticism of the Moscow Greeks— the hated heretics—or some involvement with the delicate problems of corrections of the holy texts may have been responsible for his removal from Moscow.[55]

It would seem that the most likely reason was Krizhanich's status as a catholic priest. He had gone to considerable lengths in trying to disguise his true quality. He had identified himself in Moscow as Jurii Bilish or Belish, son of Ivan, a Serbian from the town of Bihć (or Bikhch in Russian transliteration), which latter town had been in Turkish hands since 1592. He thus dissembled his origin from catholic Croatia, his own as well as his father's name (which happened to be Gaspar) and, above all, his catholic priesthood. By presenting himself as a Serbian he suggested that he belonged to the Greek Orthodox Church.[56] In Russia of the period, particularly after the Time of Troubles and the Polish invasions, membership in catholic clergy, unless covered by some official capacity, no doubt was sufficient reason in itself for arrest and deportation. Krizhanich was well aware of the danger. Twenty years earlier in his 1641 memorandum he referred to Possevino's description of the Russian practice to avoid religious disputations by sending catholic priests into permanent exile in the north and sometimes having them murdered there.[57] This knowledge does measure the intensity of Krizhanich's devotion to what he considered his life's mission. At any rate, it is more than likely, although, as far as I know, not mentioned in the large body of the relevant literature, that someone in Moscow recognized the catholic father who only eleven years earlier had some dealings with the Russian ambassador in Warsàw and then with the authorities in Moscow, when he appeared there without any disguise on his first visit in the train of the Polish embassy.[58]

Krizhanich spent fifteen long years in Siberia. He was not badly treated in Tobolsk, where he was given a very adequate sustenance and was left to work as he pleased. At that time his religion must have been fully known, because at least once he received a friendly advice from Moscow to terminate his exile by joining the Orthodox Church, an advice which he unhesitatingly rejected,[59] a significant fact for appraising the man's fundamental motives. Krizhanich was not allowed to return to Moscow until the death of Tsar Alexis in 1676. Upon his return he no longer tried to hide his quality as a priest. This alone would have rendered impossible any further pursuit of the Great Plan; and in the following year he finally obtained permission to leave Russia, which he did under the protection of the Danish ambassador, von Gabell, who undertook to deliver the fully destitute man to Rome. But Krizhanich preferred to remain in Vilno where he became a member of the Dominican Order in a new incarnation as Father Augustin. It was under this name that, a few years later, Krizhanich concluded his unsteady life in 1683, falling in or around Vienna, possibly as a chaplain in Jan Sobieski's Polish army that had come to break the Turkish siege of the city—no doubt a fitting end for a man of his convictions who in the years of his exile had copied the essay by Bellarmin on the *Ars de Bene Moriendi*, or possibly even had composed an essay of his own on the subject.

Krizhanich has been often described as an outstanding Slavophile, a great Pan-Slav. This was true of the pre-revolutionary literature, both in Russia and abroad, and is even much more so of the current writings on the subject in Soviet Russia.[60] For what follows, it is crucial to point out that this view is based on a fatal misapprehension and deflects attention from what really drove Krizhanich throughout his impetuous, adventurous, and unhappy life. It is correct that in pursuance of his plan he spoke of the union of Slavs under the scepter of the

Russian Tsar. It is also correct that he developed and wrote a curious sort of Slavic esperanto, based on a mixture of Church-Slavonic, Russian, and Croatian. But this was a natural ingredient of the 'ambages' which Krizhanich had intended to use in pursuit of his great scheme, and a hint at his future linguistic innovation is contained even in the memorandum of 1641. If advancing the cause of Pan-Slavism had been his primary aim, he could have furthered it best by joining the Orthodox Church and thereby returning from the misery of Siberian exile to a promise of influence in Moscow. But Krizhanich disdained the advice and refused to follow this course,[61] we must assume because he was above all a catholic, a priest, deeply wedded to the idea of rescuing Russia from the sinful path of the Greek heresy.

The foregoing biographical sketch would have been pointless for the purpose of this lecture, if in those years of the Siberian exile Krizhanich had not produced, along with other writings, a very considerable work under the title *Politika* or *Discourses on Government*.[62] It used to be assumed that the manuscript of the book had reached the palace library in Moscow and was possibly perused there under Tsar Alexis's successor. But modern Soviet scholarship has cast very reasonable doubts on the supposition.[63] The practical effect of the work was nil. The manuscript disappeared and was not discovered until the middle of the last century when it was published for the first time (1859).

But the importance of the book does not derive from its impact on contemporary thought and action. At one point the Congregation of Propaganda, importuned by Krizhanich's persistences and insistences, described him as '*un cervello torpido e stravagante*'—a confused and extravagant mind; on the other hand, one modern author referred to him as a 'universal genius'. He may have been both or neither. But to us he appears as a very knowledgeable person, a voracious reader,[64] who in a book written

53

far from Western libraries was able to refer to a considerable body of literature; as a man keenly interested in philology and theology as is evidenced by his writings on the subjects; and above all as an open-eyed and sharp observer of things both indigenous and alien, that is to say, Western and Russian.

In the fifteen or sixteen months which he had spent in Moscow he had noticed a great deal and he did not like what he had seen 'in this most glorious state'. He was horrified by laziness, dishonesty, and dirt, by the poor quality of goods produced, by intemperance in eating and particularly in drinking; by senseless spending on feasts and luxuries, by lack of rational accounting. And he stressed the importance of assiduous industry, supported by proper training, honesty to customers, thrift, and temperance. And in order to achieve those desirable qualities he suggested the institution of craft guilds as he had seen them in the cities of the West, with regular periods of apprenticeship and with journeymen, completing their *Wanderjahre*, and producing a master piece as a condition of becoming master. He proposed that knowledge of arithmetic should be a condition for receiving a trader's license. In addition, he suggested market controls, in particular control of weights and measures, their lack being one of the major sources of commercial deceit, which was to plague Russian economic dealings for centuries after Krizhanich's time. The air of the Russian cities did not make free, and so Krizhanich suggested that of every family of serf-peasants one of the sons should be trained as an artisan in some craft and upon acquiring competence in it, be given freedom from serfdom. Krizhanich laid great stress on Russian autocracy and wanted it to become the engine of economic reforms. But he was also conscious of the artisans' weakness *vis-à-vis* the State and argued that they must be protected against willful acts on the part of the authorities—their *krutoe vladenie* or harsh regiment.[65]

It was natural for Krizhanich to have written a book of this sort. Despite the adversity that had befallen him, he was still trying to implement his plan, or rather the first phase thereof, by imparting advice and making himself useful to the Tsar. He had greatly expanded the area of his competence. The youngster who had composed the memorandum of 1641 had never mentioned economic subjects. Nor did the memorandum contain any reference to the Germans. But in the book the hatred against the 'Germans', which notion included the English, the Scots, the Dutch, and the Swedes, is expressed time and again.

He speaks with indignation about the malicious lies which the Germans are spreading about Russian life and customs; and in this connection he includes a short chapter on Olearius whom he had undertaken to controvert while in Moscow. But the chapter turned out to be very short, and with very good reason. For many things which Olearius had criticized[66] became also the object of sharp strictures by Krizhanich himself. Propelled by his hatred, Krizhanich upbraids the Russians for their xenomania [*chuzhebesie*] and suggests a general policy of xenolasia, that is, of driving out the foreigners and of closing the frontiers, and of prohibiting Russians from traveling abroad. All this is quite inconsistent. Krizhanich might as well have referred to Olearius in support of his own position. And it was strange to see a man so much interested in economic progress wish to remove from the country the most effective agents of that progress. But the inconsistency and the strangeness disappear once it is remembered that the multinational 'Germans' were heretical protestants and their influence a clear obstacle to the union with catholic countries and the eventual conversion of Russia. It is significant that Baron Herberstein, whose description of Russia in spots was very similar to, and as unfavorable as, that of Olearius expressly gets a clean bill of health from

Krizhanich. This is natural, because Herberstein was the ambassador of his Apostolic Majesty, the Emperor Charles V.[67] To repeat, Krizhanich was and remained above all a devout catholic.

I must return now to Krizhanich's proposals and suggestions for economic reform. As we scrutinize them, it becomes quite clear that what Krizhanich aspired to was to inform the Russian artisan and trader with the positive qualities which Max Weber believed to have found in Benjamin Franklin's code of ethics. Krizhanich did not say anywhere explicitly that acquisition of those positive qualities was pleasing to the Lord, and therefore one could not say that he regarded proper economic activities to be guided by an 'ethically colored maxim' in Weber's sense. But this is beside the point. The point rather is that a man who was an ardent catholic, imbued with a deep hatred of protestantism, produced a list of *desiderata* in motivation and action which Max Weber believed to be peculiarly produced by the puritan spirit. And equally important is the fact that he did not have to invent those *desiderata* or the measures to implement them, but could simply restate what was, if not always the practice, still the ideal spirit of the towns in western Europe as it had developed there long centuries before Luther or Calvin began to reform the Church. It is not for nothing that the craft guilds received a place of honor in Krizhanich's program of economic reform.

It is easy to be confused by the multiplicity of contradictory traits evinced by the medieval cities and by the baffling regional variations. Still, when everything is said and done, their contribution, and particularly the contribution of the craft guilds, to modern industrial development must not be underestimated. They, for the first time since the fall of the Roman Empire, introduced a basic division of labor, by paring out industrial activities from the mass of agricultural production in which they had been embedded. By acquiring power and independence, the cities for the first time imparted to industrial pursuits an aura of respect, which had been entirely absent before, if we abstract from the mystery-surrounded figure of the village blacksmith. The craft guilds through their regulations and practice instilled into their members some incipient instinct of workmanship; and at the same time tended to establish some basic precepts of commercial honesty.

Max Weber could not ignore the case of the craft guilds altogether, and he referred to it, although not in his *Protestant Ethic*, but at the end of an article which he published one year later (1906).[68] The passage deserves to be quoted *in extenso*:

'In order, finally, to understand the nature of these ethical effects a last comparative remark is necessary. Also the medieval craft-guilds often revealed a supervision over the general ethical standard of their members similar to that exercised by the church discipline of the ascetic protestant sects. But the inevitable difference in the effect upon the economic behavior of the individuals is obvious. The craft-guild united members of the same craft, that is to say, competitors, and it did so in order to reduce competition and rational *Erwerbsstreben* that is inherent in it. The craft-guild performed the work of education in "bourgeois" virtues and was in a certain sense (not to be further elaborated here) a carrier of bourgeois "rationalism". But [it did so] in the sense of provision policy and traditionalism—with the well-known practical consequences insofar as its regulation of the economy became effective. The capitalistic success of a member of the craft-guild [meant] disintegration of the guild spirit—as it happened in France and England—and was abhorred. The capitalistic success of a sect brother—if achieved by righteous (*rechtlich*) means—was a proof of his vindication and grace; it enhanced the prestige and the

57

propaganda chances of the sect, and was, therefore, welcomed.'

It is true, of course, that a seventeenth-century pheno-menon stood closer to modern industrial development than an institution whose spirit was already fully dis-played at least three centuries earlier. It is furthermore true that a time came when the craft guilds became too narrow a framework for industrial development, and I shall return to the point presently. But it is equally true, as Sombart has pointed out (see above), that also puritan spirit contained obstacles to 'capitalistic' development. They, too, had to be overcome before a business spirit evolved, no longer encumbered by the specific 'ethically colored maxims', and so perfectly displayed in John Galsworthy's *Man of Property* by the silent shareholder who suddenly starts to speak, very much like the police-man *qui ne savait pas causer* in Queneau's *Zazie dans le Métro*.[69] In the process, the concept of what was 'right-eously achieved' underwent considerable changes, long before the new 'brotherhood' of cartels began to limit the competitive *Erwerbsstreben* of individual firms, and long before discriminating monopolists abandoned the prac-tice of single price which Weber also connects with the spirit of protestant sects.[70]

What Weber's passage reveals is a curious inability to appreciate the historical position of the craft guilds. The craft guild dominated medieval city was surrounded by an alien and hostile world. It had to adopt and overstress the traditional elements of equality in order to minimize the frictions and to assure the internal cohesion and unity without which the walls of the city alone would have proved altogether inadequate to protect its hard-won freedoms, its new ethics, and its economic progress. The admission that the craft guilds nurtured bourgeois 'ethical standards' and 'bourgeois rationalism' is much more dam-aging to Weber's thesis than appears from the passage.

It is not only that the 'spirit of bourgeois rationalism' does not just float *in vacuo* over the waters, but is an integral part of economic history, that is to say, that the 'spirit' of the craft guilds became embodied in their economic activities, in outputs and in the ways in which those outputs were produced. No less important is the realization that the development of the 'capitalist spirit' (if we have to use the term) is a century-long and very complex historical process, and that Weber at least should have asked the question as to how much of the spirit of the craft guilds was absorbed in the protestant ethic and how greatly its formation was thereby facilitated. In other words, instead of attributing Benjamin Franklin's code of ethics entirely to the puritan principles that had been drummed into Franklin by his puritan father in Massachusetts, Weber might well have dwelled on the striking resemblance between that code and the standards which the craft guilds in a long and painful process had instilled into the heads of their members. Had he done so, not as an afterthought at the end of a short paper, but in his principal study, a good deal less would have remained of the thesis. And it is in this sense that the Russian adventure of the 'torpid and extravagant', and yet in many respects so admirable, Croatian catholic throws a narrow but not faint ray of light on the problem and does not increase our propensity to accept Max Weber's hypothesis. Yurii Krizhanich, the learned Westerner, despised the ignorant heretical Old Believers. Yet, as far as Max Weber is concerned, the history of a great movement of religious dissent and the story of a single individual do have the same bearing and point in the same direction.

With regard to the craft guilds, however, I believe it can be said more broadly and more significantly that Russian economic history also casts some light on the great contribution of the medieval cities to the industrial history of Europe. For one cannot fail to be impressed

59

by the great differences in economic behavior between countries that did and those that did not pass through the training school of industrialization in a city which was either ruled by the craft guilds, or in which the guilds at least had acquired a position of independence and the rights of co-determination of policies. The tempo of work, liberated from the seasonal cycle of agriculture, pride in the work well-done, reliability in dealing with the customer—all these things left an indelible impact in the West. The absence of craft guilds from the economic history of Russia, or rather the feeble attempt to reproduce by a government fiat what had organically grown in the West, remained as a long-term obstacle to economic growth, to be painfully overcome in the very course of modern industrialization.[71] As will become fully clear later, I am not a believer in any necessary prerequisites of industrial development. In fact, I regard the concept of necessary prerequisites as altogether fallacious. But leaving aside the logically and historically untenable concept of necessity, it makes very good sense to regard the craft guilds in a number of European countries as having served as an *actual* prerequisite of subsequent development in those countries.

It is true, of course, that the craft guilds—once the harbinger and the vehicle of the new—in due course became an obstacle to industrial progress, seeking to subject modern enterprises to regulations and restrictions that were designed to stifle their growth. But it would be unhistorical to allow phenomena and events of a later period to merge with and blur those of an earlier period. Dialectics in general is a fairly meaningless concept as far as I am concerned. But if any positive sense at all can be attributed to it, it must surely lie in the useful warning addressed to the historian: to wit, that in the course of historical processes a given relation between the phenomena may not merely change, but change to its opposite, To stress this effect may be more in the spirit of Proudhonian anti-thetics than in that of Marxian dialectics. In any event, the role of the craft guilds in industrial history is an excellent case in point.

It may well be said that in a certain sense Krizhanich's prescriptions for the Russian economy were hopelessly antiquated. And this not only because in the seventeenth century he still advocated measures whose heyday had long passed. More important was the fact that a backward country rarely repeats step by step the road traveled by more advanced countries. And yet, Krizhanich's ideas and proposals were less irrelevant than might appear. A child of his age, he brought with him to Russia also thoughts that might be described as 'mercantilistic' and they can be discerned—inchoate and diffused, as they naturally are—mostly in his discussion of Russia's foreign trade. But this is not the crucial point. It is in a much broader and much more important sense that Krizhanich carried with him the general message of Western mercantilism. For what he proposed was a broad program for the development of the productive forces in the country, its Europeanization right down to the disappearance of the 'ugly' Russian dress and Russian beards. And he saw the autocratic State as the primary factor in the process. This makes him ideologically one of the forerunners of Peter the Great, and by the same token an anticipator of Russian mercantilism. And this leads us to the second main point to be discussed in these lectures.

3

The purpose of the following observations is to make plausible the proposition that, historically seen, the phenomenon of mercantilism can be usefully regarded as a function of the degree of economic backwardness of the countries concerned. A discussion of the Russian experience is designed to provide some evidence in support of that proposition and thereby cast some indirect light on interpretation of Western mercantilism.

Mercantilism, of course, has been, and possibly always will remain, a controversial term. Neither its nature nor its evaluation is unambiguously fixed in our minds. In fact, even the very existence of something corresponding to the term has been subject to doubt. Schumpeter, for instance, used to speak of an 'imaginary organon' or 'imaginary entity' called mercantilism[1] and he wrote quite a few pages in the relevant portions of his *History of Economic Analysis* before, either from forgetfulness or a change of mind, he stopped placing the word between deprecatory quotation marks.

Even Heckscher felt that a word on the existence of mercantilism was in order, and he argued that while mercantilism never existed in the sense in which Colbert or Cromwell did, it has specific existence as an 'instrumental concept'.[2] But this, if I may say so of a pronouncement of a man for whose work and memory I have the highest regard, is a rather trite statement. As Goethe rightly said, 'everything factual is already a theory'.[3] In other words, we cannot approach the objects of our study except by generalization and abstraction, that is to say, by 'instrumental concepts'. What we call facts or reality, including Colbert or Napoleon, are just phenomena of a low degree of abstraction. A complex of facts, be it an economic depression, say the Great Depression of the 1870s or that of the 1930s, or World War I, or British socialism, naturally is an abstraction and must be approached, or, if you wish, established, through concepts in our minds. In this sense, there is nothing specific about mercantilism. The problem is whether there are sets of concepts which yield a sufficiently large and tolerably consistent picture of reality, stressing aspects of it that for one reason or another are of interest to us.

We know, of course, very roughly what we mean when we use the term mercantilism. We have in mind, on the one hand, certain views on economic policies and the nature of the economy, and on the other, those policies themselves and the effects produced by them. Here, however, a distinction between views and policies must be made. The problem in our context is economic history. Economic policies are indeed part and parcel of economic history. But intellectual history, and with it the history of economic doctrines, may or may not belong in economic history. At times the two are inextricably connected. At times the connection is loose. My point is that regarding mercantilism from the analytical point of view has tended to make it rather difficult to perceive its role or function in economic history. And it did not make much difference whether the attitudes to mercantilist theorizing were negative or positive.

Jacob Viner following, or returning to, a tradition, dating at least since 1776, was scathing in his criticism and viewed at least the later mercantilism as a 'variety of fallacies assembled into an elaborate system of confused and self-contradictory argument'.[4] Mercantilism then was a remarkable chapter in the history of human stupidity, something written, as Erasmus used to say, *a stultis apud stultos*, by fools for fools. And indeed, how else could one describe the work of men who apparently identified wealth with precious metals, had no inkling of a self-adjusting mechanism in the balance of payments, and failed to develop the concept of a mutually beneficial trade. And on the other side, there stands Schumpeter who deals with export monopolism, exchange control, and balance of trade, and who finds that at least those [mercantilists] worthy of mention did not confuse wealth and precious metals (a completely uninteresting question, Schumpeter says, raised only by Adam Smith's 'unintelligent criticism'); that some of them perceived the price-specie flow mechanism, but doubted its effectiveness; that all mercantilist arguments were 'more or less capable of logical defense', and that there was not, or rather should not have been, any spectacular break in economic analysis from the 'embryonic fund of theoretical knowledge' of the mercantilists.[5] And then there is Keynes's point that in the peculiar circumstances of the time, given stability of the wage unit and of liquidity preference, the interest in the influx of precious metals was well justified.[6] And finally, there were in the 1930s a few popularizers of Keynes who did not hesitate to regard mercantilism in the light of the policies of the Great Depression as a system designed to achieve full employment.

My point is not that Viner's strictures, or Keynes's general interpretation, or Schumpeter's rather more detailed investigation are in any sense wrong in themselves. Nor can it be gainsaid that there were rather obvious inconsistencies in mercantilistic thought. This is not the issue at all. My point rather is that concentrating on the theoretical or quasi-theoretical views of the mercantilists and gauging the degree of their stupidity or intelligence, as the case may be, does not open up the proper avenue for appraising mercantilism as a significant sequence of events in economic history.

By contrast, as one turns to the work of economic historians such as Cunningham and Schmoller, but above all to Heckscher, both a general historical interpretation of mercantilism and a specific problem of that interpretation becomes possible. In saying that, I have in mind primarily Heckscher's and his predecessors' view of basic ends of mercantilist policies. Heckscher describes the historical period of mercantilism as the timespan lying between the Middle Ages and the *laissez-faire* era.[7] This is not only a temporal limitation, but also a substantive determination, and this in more than just one sense. This is first of all the period in which falls the formation of developed statehoods, which, incidentally, may or may not have been 'nation-states'.[8] It is, second, a period which partakes of both medieval and modern elements. It was therefore natural for Cunningham to see the increase in the power of the aggressive expanding State, seeking its natural, or unnatural boundaries, involved in continual warlike enterprises, as the primary aim of contemporaneous policies; and to view economic policies as essentially subordinate to that aim.[9]

Once this is done, no doubt many aspects of mercantilistic policies appear altogether comprehensible. If precious metals are needed to keep the war chests full, a policy aiming at export surpluses is reasonable. If power is the aim, mutually beneficial trade which enriches also the enemies is undesirable. And above all, foreign trade and foreign economic relations are but one and not necessarily the most important aspect of economic policies. What matters most is development of the domestic economy in such a fashion as to make it able to support effectively the power aspirations of the government. An integral part of such economic policy are measures designed to overcome the medieval localism by converting the State territory into an economically unified area. Indeed, the policies of unification deserved a central place within the complex of mercantilistic policies, and Heckscher quite understandably devoted the whole first volume of his work to the relevant measures: construction of roads and canals, abolition of tolls on roads and rivers, creation of unified systems of weights and measures as well as currency; issuance of uniform industrial regulations for the territory of the State, involving among other things rewriting some of the industrial policies of the medieval towns on a national level. Here, however, lies the problem.

There is little doubt that Heckscher was keenly alive to the crucial role of power in the mercantilistic policies. He understood well, in contrast to some of his critics, that power in the mercantilistic State was something essentially different from power in a *laissez-faire* State, although quite similar to that in modern dictatorships. Heckscher had learned well the lesson taught by his teacher Harald Hjärne, a very considerable Swedish historian, that power of the mercantilist type is maintained through its continued exercise, so that regimentation has a value in itself, apart from the aims it is designed to achieve.[10]

And yet, despite his lucid understanding of the role of power as a determining motivation of policies, Heckscher in his treatment of mercantilism did not deal with the policy of unification as with something that was clearly subordinated to the overriding aim to maintain and to increase the power of the State. Rather, he placed the two goals, as it were, on a par beside each other. The reason, I believe, is fairly clear. Heckscher could not fail to be impressed by the fact that wealth as an independent end seemed to compete with power effectively. Time and again, he felt, he had to weaken his emphasis on power in favor of opulence. But this raises a general problem which is directly pertinent to our subject: Europe and Russia.

The concept of *Europe* is basic to Heckscher's *Mercantilism*. In this regard Hjärne's influence upon Heckscher was perhaps most obvious. Hjärne's approach to history was determined by his basic belief in the unity of the European civilization. The Greek legacy, absorbed in

66

Christianity, the Church, and the Empire of the Middle Ages had created a homogeneous Europe as a cultural entity which the modern system of sovereign States had transformed but not eradicated, the system rather than its members being considered by Hjärne as the fundamental reality. Despite all anarchy, Europe through long centuries had grown to be a 'real historical community'.[11] As a result, Hjärne felt, historical problems of individual countries could not be meaningfully treated except against the background of the European community as a whole. It was probably quite natural for Hjärne, who was deeply interested in the history of international political relations, to develop this particular emphasis. The concept of the *communauté du droit des gens*, of the *Abendlaendisch-Christliche Gemeinschaft*, of the family of nations, for a long time was traditionally regarded as the central concept of international law.[12]

It was this message which Hjärne's students received. Heckscher heard it first when as a boy of fifteen he attended Hjärne's summer-school lectures in Uppsala, and he retained it to the end of his days. It is clearly reflected in his *Mercantilism*. The book, he says, was designed to be 'a contribution to the history of economic policy as a *common European problem*'.[13] As a result, Heckscher deals with the problem of mercantilism 'by selecting typical aspects in the economic policy of typical countries'.[14] This is a crucial statement both for the methodology and the criticism of the book. It is based on the view that 'when all is said, economic development followed similar lines all over the world';[15] the world presumably meaning the world of Europe.

Here lies both the strength and the weakness of Heckscher's approach. If the development was perfectly uniform everywhere, then every country is a 'typical country' and the choice in concentrating on this or that area lies mainly in differences regarding availability of information. Beyond that it can be only special interests

67

of the student in a given area that lead him to exploring the peculiarities of development in that area. But such study can only widen and not deepen our understanding of the general phenomenon. I believe that this position is unsatisfactory. Generalized patterns must be formed on the basis of general information, and the expectation should be that as a result two things happen. On the one hand, the general concept, Heckscher's 'instrumental tool', is likely to change and, moreover, the pattern itself is likely to become less homogeneous than it appeared on the basis of a more restricted area of study. In other words, the problem is a re-appraisal of both the *genus* and the *species*, a re-appraisal that should lead not just to definitional and morphological clarification, but also to a causal explanation.

To find generally applicable elements in a given sequence and interrelation of events does not in itself preclude great spatial divergences. More or less stress can be laid on the development in the individual areas. One of the most characteristic features of Heckscher's book is the relatively narrow scope assigned in it to such differences. To be sure, a good deal is said on policy differences between France and England with regard to practice of industrial regulations, and from time to time brief references are made to still other deviations in countries like Germany and Austria. What matters is that there is no attempt to bring those differences into a systematic form, thus providing an explanation for them.

And beyond that there is an area that remained almost entirely outside the scope of Heckscher's treatment. And that is Russia. Again, Hjärne's influence may have been responsible for this failure. Hjärne was indeed a student of Russian history, but he was driven into concern with Russia by his studies of the period of Charles XII. He did not consider Russia a member of the European community, and, in fact, he viewed the problem of Russo-Swedish relations of the period as a decision on Russia's admission to that community. Here may lie the source of Heckscher's reluctance to turn to Russia while he was investigating a common *European* problem. As we have seen before, the question whether Russia was or was not 'Europe' remained a moot one, not only after the ticket of admission was acquired at the battlefield of Poltava and at the negotiation table at Nystadt, but, more importantly, after the reform work of Peter the Great who in the annals of Russia is usually described as the Tsar *Preobrazovatel'* which does not mean reformer, but transformer. For our purposes, however, the question cannot be answered on the basis of general cogitations about cultural legacy or increasing or decreasing weight in the concert of powers. If mercantilism is a phenomenon of economic policies, the answer must come from an understanding of those policies.

Turning now to Russian mercantilist experience, I propose to deal exclusively with the reforms of Peter the Great. To confine the presentation in this fashion does not imply that Peter had no predecessors. Some elements of his policies no doubt were visible during the successive reigns of his father, brother, and sister. In the more remote past certain similarities can be discerned in the second half of the sixteenth century. But those inchoate attempts rather pale into insignificance when compared with what followed them. I know that continuity is an 'O.K. word' with historians. Continuity, however, is a term that has more meanings than its users are usually aware of, and so has its antonym of discontinuity.[16] If we use the term in the sense of a sudden change in the rate of change—meaning a kink in the curve of investment and output—then there is no doubt that the first quarter of the eighteenth century in Russia was marked by a momentous discontinuity. It opened a new chapter in the economic history of the country.

Militarily, the period was marked by continual wars,

even though the intensity of the conflicts varied. Over-shadowing the wars against the Turks—one victory and one ignominious defeat in which the fruits of the earlier conquest were lost—and saying nothing of the Persian war—there was the Great Northern War which started with the Russian debacle at Narva (1700), lasted for most of the reign, and eventually put an end to Sweden's *stormaktstiden*, the Swedish Age of Empire. Viewed from the shores of the Atlantic Ocean, Sweden may not have stood in the forefront of Western civilization, but for Russia this was the struggle against the West, against an enemy immensely superior in culture, both spiritual and material. In the process of Russian expansion this was the crucial drive to the open seas, that is to say, the push towards the West into Europe. The Black Sea proved unattainable, for the time being, but the Baltic, which Ivan the Terrible had craved, but could not hold, was the object of the war and the prize of victory. But while the task facing the Russian govern-ment—or, more personally, the Russian autocrat—was modern in the contemporaneous sense of involving him in a conflict with a modern power, all the resources at his disposal were abysmally backward. The problem, there-fore, was to lift the military and economic potential of the country to a level more consonant with the nature of the task. In principle, this was the standard mercan-tilistic situation. In dealing with the economic policies of the Petrine State, I have to point out first the standard ingredients of mercantilism and then touch on its specific Russian aspects.

There is first of all the unification policy. Administra-tively, pre-Petrine Russia had already been centralized to an astonishing degree. Still Peter's administrative reforms greatly tightened the grip of the government over the territory of the State. Weights and measures became more uniform; some old measures were abolished, others were adjusted, as were some measures of length in order to accommodate the foot and the inch which Peter brought to Russia from his trip to England. By contrast, no attempt was made to remove the internal duties. They were not abolished until nearly three decades after Peter's death (1753). This, however, is not surprising. The Renaissance monarchy in France at times even raised the internal tolls and tariffs, the fiscal needs seeming more important than the goal of unification.[17] It is such conflicts and inconsistencies, including that between investment and military expenditures (see below), that bedevil simplistic views of mercantilism which are indeed vulnerable to criticism. But inconsistencies of this sort essentially reveal instability of time horizons of statesmen, and they need not detract from the validity of broad interpretations. But physical unification—the problem of communications—was given great attention. Roads and bridges were built. So were canals. The Baltic Sea was linked with the Caspian by a system that hit the River Volga rather far upstream, but still provided an essential connection with the eastern tributaries of the Volga and, by the same token, with the mines and mills of the Ural Mountains. The project to connect the Baltic with the Asov and Black seas by a Volga–Don canal was begun, but remained unfinished; but the canal around Lake Lagoda was started as the first step to other and more effective inland waterways between the Neva and the Volga basin, although its construction took longer than anticipated and its completion did not occur before 1732.

As in the West, there was the previously-mentioned problem of choice between immediate war expenditures and investment outlays to provide the basis for larger military resources after some lapse of time. This was the Colbert–Louvois dilemma. There are some indications in the papers of the Tsar that he was aware of the problem. But it is precisely at this point that something *sui generis* becomes visible in the Russian experience. For the impression that one receives, particularly from actions during the first part of the reign, say until 1715, is that the answer to the problem was not a calculated allocative decision, but the daimonic feeling that development was a function of will power translated into pressure and compulsion. The result was the simultaneity of effort in all directions: constructing and equipping the navy; building harbors; creating a new capital in the swamps of the Neva estuary; prospecting for minerals, opening mines and erecting blast furnaces and building factories, even though when it comes to plants that really deserve the name, the numbers were much less than had been assumed by earlier historians;[18] and at the same time reorganizing and re-arming the army and reshaping the administrative machinery of the government. The new civil service was designed to push, press, and squeeze, to overcome resistance, indolence, and dishonesty, except that the deeply-ingrained habits of government graft and corruption ate their ways into the new machinery, however ready the Tsar's whip, or rather the heavy cudgel he favored, was to fall on the shoulders of the guilty dignitaries—the fledglings from Peter's nest, to use Pushkin's phrase—to say nothing of torture to which some of them were submitted, of prisons to which they were sent, and of gallows on which they ended.

The very magnitude of the effort, its vigor, amplitude, and persistence endow the Petrine reign with unique features. Nowhere else in the mercantilistic world do we encounter a comparable case of a great spurt, compressed within such a short period. Nowhere else was the starting point so low; nowhere else were the obstacles that stood in the path of development so formidable. And along with differences in the vehemence of the process were the differences in its character. Nowhere else was the State to any comparable extent the demiurgos of economic development. Nowhere else was it so strongly dominated by the interests of the State.[19] Hence came the composition of the nascent industry with its concentration above all on production and working of metals as well as on plants producing uniforms for the army, sails, ropes, and timber for the ships, and powder for the guns.[20] Hence it came that the large-scale plants were established and run—at least for some time—by the State; that for those plants the State supplied everything: land and entrepreneurship and management, capital and labor (about which something more will be said presently), and, finally, the demand. It is true that at times, in a sudden flight of fancy, Peter would order the establishment of a factory producing Venetian mirrors or of a workshop producing Gobelin tapestries, but those short-lived although costly escapades must be seen as aberrations from a goal that in general was pursued with unswerving constancy. The *manufactures royales* in France did cater to the luxury demand of the Court where that demand served an important social and political function: the splendor of the Court was to reconcile the nobility to its loss of power to the monarchy. In Prussia, much poorer than France, the problem, during a certain period, was solved by granting the Junkers increasing rights over the peasantry and by appeasing them in this fashion. But in Russia the problem did not exist at all. The Russian State was poor but strong.

The combination of poverty and strength of the State resulted in pressures that were incomparably greater than those produced by mercantilistic policies in other countries. The budgetary revenues were but one of the forms these pressures took, but the fiscal policies reveal them with particular clarity. The bulk of the revenue came from direct taxes and the internal tariffs, the latter partly being in the nature of a sales tax and even a turnover tax. But nothing indicates the desperate urge of the government to squeeze additional money out of the population than the crop of new indirect taxes. An immense amount of ingenuity went into designing them. A new office—

that of *pribyl'shchiki*, literally 'profiteers', that is, people working for the profit of the State—was created. Those were men whose job it was to suggest new revenues. It was one of them who had the idea—speedily put into effect—that every petition to the authorities was to be written on a special paper with an eagle stamped upon it, the petitioner having to pay for the value of the stamp. The requirement of this 'eagle paper', incidentally, remained on the statute book until the revolution of 1917. Everything imaginable was taxed: watering horses and beehives, peasants' private bathhouses and their beards as well as 'illegal', that is, 'un-German', dress of people in the towns. It is doubtful whether all these flights of fiscal imagination actually produced results that were consonant with the effort involved in inventing and collecting these taxes. According to Miliukov, the 'eagle paper' in 1724 brought about two per mille of total revenue and the proceeds of taxes on dress and beards amounted to about one-quarter of one per mille of the total.[21] But no source of revenue, however small, was disdained. The fiscal edifice was finally crowned in the penultimate year of the reign by the introduction of a poll tax or 'soul tax' based on regular censuses of the population, this tax, too, remaining in force for nearly 160 years. The precise evolution of the tax burden over the period of the reign is still a matter of controversy. A well-known Soviet economist, Strumilin, even argued that it was lower per head in 1724 than it had been in 1680.[22] But this extreme position is based on very questionable computations and the only thing that can be concluded from the debate is that the rise in the per capita tax burden, while perhaps somewhat less than that computed by Miliukov in his standard study of Peter's budget, was still disastrously large.[23]

Strumilin, for rather obvious reasons, is at pains to show that Peter's reforms did not lead to a 'ruination' [*razorenie*] of the Russian peasantry. It should be noted first that the tax burden of 1680 was already intolerably heavy, and Kliuchevskii said with reference to that year that 'the paying forces of the population had been stressed beyond the point of exhaustion'.[24] On the other hand, it is natural that after the end of the Northern War (1721) some relief of the tax burden, as compared with the previous years, could, and in fact had to, take place. But a comparison between 1680 and 1724, interesting as it may be for some reasons, is of limited importance when the problem is to measure the weight of the fiscal burden imposed upon the peasantry during the first two decades of the eighteenth century. Using wherever possible data contained in Strumilin's study and making most conservative assumptions, I have computed the tax burden at the beginning of the second decade of the century, that is, *after* the decisive victory at Poltava in 1709, as amounting to sixty-four percent of the grains harvested from the peasant household's allotment of arable land. This is surely a most shocking result, and whatever admiration Strumilin felt for the great achievements of the 'Transformer' on the throne, should not have prevented him from making a similar computation. I may be not wrong in assuming that this making light of the disastrous cost to the people was designed to suggest and justify the inference that also Stalin's superindustrialization and collectivization policies were altogether tolerable.[25]

Yet, compulsion went far beyond confiscation of a huge portion of the population's income which even Strumilin—very implausibly in the light of his own data —believes to have been around twenty per cent of total national income.[26] Also twenty percent would be quite excessive in a country where the standard of living was probably below anything that would have been considered subsistence minimum in the West. Supply of manpower for army and navy, for construction projects for mines and factories, for forest work and transportation

75

was the area where brute force was most clearly displayed. The Tsar's lack of concern for the cost of his projects in terms of human lives was absolute. It may be an exaggeration that hundreds of thousands of workers perished in the construction of the—subsequently lost— port of Taganrog on the Sea of Azov, but the figure was plausible enough for a qualified acceptance by Kliuchevskii. And similar statements were made of the Baltic ports.[27] It is probably natural that horrors of this sort appear to be of little weight to people of Strumilin's ilk who have lived through the contemporary experience of the Soviet industrialization.[28]

As in the West, there were the stern measures against vagrants and beggars.[29] Even in this respect, the Petrine State went one better on the West by attempting to punish not only the receiver, but also the giver of alms, a step that was bound to remain ineffective in a country where a beggar was considered to be a representative of Christ and possibly Christ himself. But the impressment of beggars represented only one aspect of the labor policy, even though in the factories in Moscow and two other cities (Yaroslavl' and Kazan') in the 1730s more than twenty-one percent of the labor force apparently had been beggars before being brought to the factory.[30] Year by year, orders went out to local authorities all over the newly-established nine provinces of the huge country to send men—State peasants—to places many hundreds of miles from their native villages. Mines and factories received whole villages assigned to them, many of those villages located far away from the place of employment. In the later part of the reign the government began to transfer mines and factories into private hands; individuals had to take them over whether they wanted to do so or not, or as Peter put it, 'be it willingly or unwillingly'.[31] Thus even the private entrepreneur—so unlike the Schumpeterian image of him—could be, and at times was, created by appointment, by a fiat of the State, just as Molière's Sganarelle was made a *médecin malgré lui* by having been beaten with a big stick. It was in this later period (1721) that the private entrepreneurs were given the right to purchase villages of serfs, the latter to be tied permanently to the factories.

There has been a debate going on among the Soviet historians as to whether the enterprises established under Peter were capitalistic or feudal.[32] The faith in the usefulness of such ambiguous labels is more remarkable for its childlike quality than for its explanatory power. There is no doubt that skilled labor—masters and foremen—imported from abroad were contractual workers who earned very high wages and were extremely well-treated. Many of them proved ignorant and inept, quite unworthy of their hire. Some of those who came were just the jetsam and flotsam of foreign shores. But Peter did not follow the angry advice he received to send such men away in disgrace. Foreigners were needed, and there should be no tales told abroad about their ill treatment in Russia. Krizhanich may have been Peter's forerunner, but the xenolasia of the learned Croatian priest was altogether foreign to Peter whose concern for economic development was not blurred by ulterior motives.

By contrast, native workers were exposed to an entirely different treatment, both with regard to income and personal freedom. Even to the extent that so-called free labor was used, the adjective must be taken with the greatest possible caution. There is a regrettable tendency of some Soviet historians to speak of free labor as soon as a wage was paid. Apprentices were tied to the factory for seven years plus three more years after the completion of their apprenticeship. More importantly, delinquent debtors were sent to the mines, if they were able-bodied males (old people and minors, who as heirs also could be delinquent debtors, were to be put to less strenuous jobs); if they were females, they were dispatched to the weaving sheds.[33] Criminals of both sexes naturally were used as heavy laborers. Prostitutes were sentenced to labor 'without limit of time and if necessary until death'.[34] What mattered more was that time and again large numbers of artisans were forcibly collected in Moscow and other towns and sent to the Urals. A salter could ask the government for delivery of 9,000 laborers and, after some bargaining, receive 5,000. Year in, year out, ukazes were issued ordering mobilization of 40,000 workers to be sent, under guard to St Petersburg from all over the country, including Siberia; while the home villages and home towns of the laborers were held to pay for their sustenance. Thousands of artisans were forcibly brought to St Petersburg for permanent settlement.[35] At times promises were made designed to attract contractually-hired labor to factories and other projects, but when, later on, the census for the poll tax caught the so-called free workers in factories, they were subsequently tied to the factories for good, that is to say, enserfed.[36] Children of soldiers as well as older soldiers were forcibly used as laborers, the service of a soldier in the Petrine army and afterwards being for lifetime and ending only with incapacity by illness or old age. Strumilin must admit that 'after 1726 in state factories also recruits conscripted beyond the military needs of the army were added to the labor force'. 'But', he goes on to say, 'they received wages just as other workers and fulfilled the same functions as the others.'[37] By this line of reasoning also a peasant serf put into a gentry factory and given money to keep body and soul together would be regarded as a freely-hired laborer and the enterprise would become a 'capitalist' enterprise. This is a fairly foolish position, stubbornly maintained in order to make a rather irrelevant point. What matters, of course, are not terminological quibbles, but the historical fact that it was the power of the State that was used in the historical process of creating the industrial labor force. Wage or no wage, the labor was essentially a coerced, forced labor, created as an industrial labor force by the fiat of the State. It is not surprising, therefore, that most of the mines and factories looked like fortresses and were guarded by detachments of soldiers in order to prevent escapes.

Nor is it surprising that industrial labor should be essentially unfree labor in a State that was a 'service state', or as the Russian phrase runs, a 'serfdom state'. For it was not only the peasantry that was enserfed to the gentry. The gentry, created by the State, was under the obligation to serve the State, and the serfdom of the peasantry had a clear social function, that is, to pay for the services of the gentry, both military and civil. By serving the gentry the peasant was serving the State. Therefore also the never-ending cogitations of Marxian historians in Russia about the class nature of the Petrine State—was it a gentry State or was it a merchants' State? —miss the essential fact that the State was not the State of this or that class. It was the State's State.

The Marxian approach which has yielded extremely useful insights in appropriate periods and circumstances —say England of the nineteenth century or Austria in the interwar period, to illustrate at random—becomes altogether sterile when applied to the Russian demiurgos State. Marxism at all times had difficulty with explaining dictatorial power. Even when, as in the case of Napoleon III, the State that was not dominated by a certain class could be presented as *originating* from an equilibrium of class power, the problem still remained that once the dictatorial State was established, it was able to pursue an independent policy of its own, because it had become a power in its own right. Engels, who created the 'theory' of equilibrium of class forces, was at pains to present such equilibria as 'exceptional', situations arising from the special conditions of a moment ['*momentan*'].[38] Even Engels's own examples, which include two centuries of absolute monarchy, do not fit his definition too well. But when it comes to Russia, it is not only that the use of terms such as 'exception' or 'moment' is patently unsuitable to characterize the course of Russian history and the role of the State in it. The overriding consideration is that it would make little sense to regard the autocratic State as emerging from equilibrium of class power. It was not class power relations that created the State. The obverse was true: it was the State that was creating the classes: labor, and even the entrepreneurs, although soon more and more men became ready to make use voluntarily of the great benefits that were held out to them by the State. And even though the State did not create the peasantry, it was the policy of the State through its methods of repression, its passport system, introduced by Peter, as well as its fiscal arrangements which kept the peasantry put and tended to reduce, though not to stop, its escape from oppression into the wide open spaces of the East.[39] But without classes as independent forces, the materialistic conception of history becomes sterile because the phenomenon of the independent State involves the primacy of the political rather than of the economic factor, the latter playing an instrumental role in the service of the former. Marxism in general found it difficult to place the mercantilistic State within its conceptual framework, but the degree of the difficulty varied from country to country, reaching its maximum in Russian mercantilism.

Before I proceed to summarize the comparison of Russian mercantilism with that of the West, I must refer to an aspect of the former that was, by contrast to others, not more but less in evidence in Russia. I am referring to the fact that the Russians, among their manifold borrowings from the West, did not include the Western preoccupation with foreign trade and precious metals. To some extent, this is reflected in the lexical changes in the Russian language and a word thereon may be in order. As a result of the intensive borrowing from abroad, things never seen before and often even never heard of

before made their appearance in Russia. New things—
and concepts—required new words, and the language was
therefore flooded with foreign words, very frequently
quite imperfectly Russified. It is interesting to note then
that of some 3,500 foreign words that entered the language during Peter's reign about one quarter of them
were shipping terms; another quarter was occupied by
terms connected with government administration; the
third quarter was held by military terminology; the balance was taken up by miscellaneous words with a pre-
ponderance of luxury terms imported from France, either
directly or via Germany and Poland. But what is striking
is the absence of both economic terms and business
terminology. There were perhaps two dozen borrowed
words which could be stretched to suit the concept. In
particular, accounting terms were missing altogether.
This is as it should be. The economic enterprises created
during the Petrine spurt were not oriented toward any
careful calculus of costs and revenues. The State, that is,
the Russian people, were to foot the bill, and profit-
ability or its absence aroused little interest.[40] The ingenuity of the previously mentioned 'profiteers' that
went into invention of new minute taxes, each of them
requiring special collecting apparatus, was not matched
by a comparable endeavor in the sphere of industry,
except, of course, for the perennial struggle against deceit
and corruption. Incidentally, the 'profiteers' themselves
often showed excessive interest in their private profits.
One of them died on the wheel for taking bribes and the
inventor of 'eagle's paper', the king of the profiteers, died
in prison before his trial for the same offense.[41]

Very similarly, no terms were allowed to enter the
Russian language from the mercantilist literature of the
time. And indeed the interest in foreign trade and the
balance of payments as well as in precious metals was
clearly subordinated to the problem of economic development and foreign policies. An active balance of trade was

indeed a matter of considerable importance. The export surplus was to finance the subsidies and bribes given to allies in the war against Sweden. It was needed to pay the foreign technicians. Foreign trade in a number of basic commodities (the so-called forbidden goods, such as potash, caviare, rhubarb, ship timber, furs, and others) was maintained as a government export monopoly, although most of those commodities were released to private trade in 1719. There were some import prohibitions, mostly directed against luxury goods, and there were some very loosely-enforced measures of control of movement of precious metals. At one point Peter tried to find out in which way foreign prohibitions against exports of precious metals could be evaded. In addition, there was throughout concern for the terms of trade, and particularly for the low prices offered for Russian goods by foreign traders in Russia. Peter tried to order establishment of merchant companies in Russia, precisely in order to raise export prices, but did not pursue the matter and the project bore no fruit. But at no time did Peter in this field exhibit the boundless energy which was so characteristic of his actions elsewhere. Essentially, it was only in the last years of Peter's life, particularly after his visit to France, that foreign trade began to attract more serious attention, resulting in the first protectionist tariff in which the degree of protection varied directly with the ratio of domestic output to total consumption, the duty rising up to seventy-five percent *ad valorem*.[42] This was the very opposite of an infant industry tariff and probably reflected the high cost of output in those branches of industry on the development of which greatest emphasis had been placed in the preceding years. It is reasonable to assume that those industries were subject to increasing rather than decreasing cost, and in some way the tariff, crude as it was, may have been broadly adjusted to such patterns of quantitative restrictions of imports as existed prior to its introduction. The main point, however, is the one previously made. Something that seemed to stand in the very focus of Western mercantilist thought appears to have played a very subordinate role in Russia.

A distinctive feature of Russian mercantilism was the almost complete absence in it of general theorizing. At the beginning of this century social policies in Australia were once described as *socialisme sans doctrine*. Similarly, the Petrine policies were *mercantilisme sans doctrine*. But one of a couple of exceptions to this proposition may be mentioned here, because it tends to confirm the conclusion just reached. The reference is to the curious literary document of the period, composed by Ivan Pososhkov —*The Book on Poverty and Wealth*.[43] Soviet and also some pre-Soviet enthusiasts liked to describe Pososhkov as one of the great economists of all times.[44] This is fairly ludicrous. But the book of this auto-didact of peasant origin is remarkable in many respects and may be considered the only contemporaneous comprehensive mercantilistic tract on Russian economic policies, as one may well abstract from the memoranda of F. S. Saltykov, who was influenced by his long residence abroad. It is, therefore, instructive to observe Pososhkov's distribution of emphasis.

Pososhkov does indeed deal with foreign trade. He is interested in improving the country's terms of trade by exerting pressures on foreign merchants. In the process, he incidentally assumes very low price elasticity of foreign demand for Russian goods, and obversely very high price elasticity of Russian demand for foreign commodities. He is interested in expanding the volume of Russian exports and applies an infant industry argument of sorts to them by suggesting that exporting at a loss for some time will be profitable in the long run. On the import side he calls for drastic steps against luxury goods and at one point even objects to purchases of foreign cloth for soldiers' uniforms, despite the existing price differentials, arguing in this and in a couple of other cases the advantage of keeping money at home. But all this is far from playing a central part in his argument. The balance of trade is never mentioned explicitly and there is never the remotest hint that the export surplus as such is the source of the country's increase in wealth. For Pososhkov's main interest is directed to problems of economic development.

Here the range of subjects he treats is very wide: training of workers; improvement in the quality of products and introduction of severe penalties for shoddy goods; technical innovations and protection of inventors; location of industries, with regard to which he, curiously enough, considers cheapness of food as exercising the strongest pull in determining the place of production;[45] development of chemical industry; suggestions for efficient prospecting for minerals; criticism of inefficiency in collecting indirect taxes and proposals for reform of Peter's direct taxation of peasants so as to increase the State's revenues. It was in the latter connection that he issued to the gentry a stern warning not to exploit the peasantry excessively with a clear understanding of the existing competition for the product of peasant labor— and for that labor itself—between the State and the gentry. What in fact was intimated was a threat of 'reversion' [*reduktionen*] of gentry lands to the crown upon the then recent Swedish model.[46] Pososhkov said: 'The landlords [*pomeshchiki*] are not permanent owners of the peasants. Their direct owner is the autocrat of all the Russias, and the landlords possession is a temporary one ...' And Pososhkov went on to say that peasants must be protected by imperial edicts, because 'the wealth of the peasantry is the wealth of the Tsar'.[47] Pososhkov made a number of suggestions designed to improve the lot of the peasantry, so as to prevent the peasants' flights 'southward and to the border regions, and even beyond the frontiers, populating foreign territories and leaving their own land empty'.[48]

There is more, however, to Pososhkov's book than the important priority assigned in it to economic development. The book was finished in 1724, a short time before Peter's death. By that time, Russia's position as a great power had been assured, but at the cost of an effort that —very visibly to the eyes of contemporaries—had led to the impoverishment of the country. Hence came Pososhkov's insistence that continuation of economic development must be accompanied by increases in popular well-being.

A specific Russian pattern of economic development was reaching completion. And in this sense Pososhkov's book, while characteristic of Russian mercantilism, bears the mark of a precise historical moment in its evolution. We have, of course, no proper statistics to measure the speed of industrial growth during Peter's reign, let alone what happened to national income over the period. Even the estimates of the growth of pig iron are quite uncertain. Still, it may be assumed that it had grown at about eight percent per year between 1700 and 1725.[49] It is most unlikely that any other industrial commodity could boast a similarly high rate of growth. But even if we assume the whole industrial establishment to have grown at the same rate, such an increase in what after all still was a tiny portion of the total economy was compatible with great reductions in national income, the disposable incomes of the population decreasing even more. What certainly increased was the wealth of the State that was designed to support the power of the State. As Kliuchevskii put it: the State grew fatter and fatter and the people grew leaner and leaner. The great historian was referring to the seventeenth century, but his pithy conclusion fits the Petrine period with particular force.

In attempting to draw conclusions from the preceding discussion of Russian mercantilism, the following points appear to stand out:

1) if we wish to conceive of mercantilism as a common

European phenomenon, it is power policies and sub-ordination of economic policies to the exigencies of power that provide the common denominator; the economic policies centering on economic development in general, and industrial development in particular;

2) for the rest we observe deviations from the basic pattern. The role of vested interests in co-determining the policies of the state varied from country to country. In viewing the Petrine experience no one possibly could claim with Adam Smith that 'the sneaking arts of under-ling tradesmen have been erected into political maxims'[50] or that 'the merchants and manufacturers have been by far the principal architects . . . of this whole mercantile system.'[51] They were the objects rather than the agents of Petrine policies. Even so, the emphasis on foreign trade, active balance of trade and the resulting influx of precious metals, and, finally, protectionism was enor-mously strong in some countries and tended to be fairly insignificant in others;

3) in dealing with deviations of this kind, it is possible simply to register them as such and let it go at that. Then the economic history of Europe appears in a rather fragmentized fashion, the deviations greatly detracting from, and even destroying, the unity that was so dear to Heckscher and his teacher. Yet something more can be said on the subject. As one reviews once more in one's mind the history of the Petrine era in Russia and looks for reasons for the overwhelming role of the State, the ubiquitousness of compulsion, the weakness of vested interests, and the single-minded concentration on power, the economic backwardness of the country surely suggests itself as the main, if not the sole, explanatory factor. But if this be true, then the Russian experience does provide a clue to the understanding of mercantilism westward beyond the borders of Russia. The intensity of the deviations from the basic pattern, beginning from the greater role of vested interests and the consideration

of wealth as an independent goal of policies are then to be regarded as a function of the decreasing backwardness of the countries concerned. If this proposition holds, as I believe it does, then it becomes possible to arraign mercantilistic countries according to the degree of their economic backwardness, starting probably with the Low Countries and continuing over England and France to Prussia, and finally, Russia. If the resulting picture should be one of a fair degree of continuity in the sense of gradual increase in the significance of the basic pattern until the naked power point is reached in the east of the continent, then indeed the European economic history in the mercantilist period may be conceived as a unity, although not a uniform, homogeneous unity, but a diversified, graduated unity, which, however, is comprehensible as such because of its relation to the degree of economic backwardness which serves not only as an organizing but also as an explanatory principle.

Assuming that this view of European development in the mercantilist period is at all defensible, it would seem to accomplish two things: it conceives of Russia as a part of Europe and by the same token it uses Russian history to add to our understanding of the economic history of Europe. It constitutes an attempt to move backward in time my general conception of European industrial development in the more modern period, that is to say, in the eighteenth and nineteenth centuries. But before addressing myself to the question as to how Russian industrial development in the later period may help us to understand the industrial development in the West, one final point must be made concerning Russian mercantilism with regard to its effects on the country's subsequent development.

Heckscher's well-balanced and judicious appraisal of mercantilism emphasizes both the contrast and the concord between mercantilism and *laissez-faire*. Leaving aside the field of intellectual history, the field of doctrines

87

and ideology, and riveting our sight to economic processes, it may indeed be said that in the West in some
respects mercantilist policies prepared the soil for modern
industrial development while in others they had created
obstacles that had to be removed, at times requiring a
considerable effort. Incidentally, some of those obstacles
may have originally been in the nature of factors promoting rather than retarding economic development. Let
me repeat what I have said at the end of the previous
lecture. Whatever the meaning of Marxian dialectics and,
as we know, it is quite elusive, if it means among other
things that in the course of historical development the
nature of something that for some time had a positive
effect, may over a rather short time change to its opposite, this is a most useful reminder which an historian
will ignore at his own peril.

I am not in a position to demonstrate here how the
problem of obstacles created by mercantilist policies
actually presented itself in the individual countries of
Europe. But I should like to volunteer a general hypothesis and then say a few words on the conditions in
Russia in this respect. The general proposition, or rather
a surmise, I can offer is this: the less backward, economically speaking, was a country when it went through
its mercantilist experience, the less formidable were the
obstacles for subsequent development that resulted from
that experience and the more easily they were overcome.

Let me try to illustrate: the Austrian monarchy undoubtedly occupied an intermediate position with regard
to its economic backwardness between Russia and the
West. In Austria, Joseph II (1780–90) was the great
mercantilist on the throne, the man who liked to say that
every single thread of the clothes he wore on his back
came from indigenous material and labor. One of the
outstanding features of Josephine policies, greatly in-
tensifying those pursued by Maria Theresa, was unification. 'The whole Monarchy will become one mass of

people ruled in the same fashion',[52] he wrote to his brother. But unification meant, first and foremost, the creation of a strong centralized state. In the process the power of the bureaucratic machinery was greatly increased, most notably at the expense of the gentry diets and its local apparatus in the individual provinces, both German and non-German. There is little doubt that these policies under Joseph II favored the economic development of the country and facilitated the introduction and enforcement of economic reforms. But when in the nineteenth century the enlightened despotism of Joseph was replaced, in the period of reaction between 1815–48, by the unenlightened despotism of Metternich, and economic progress began to be viewed with great suspicion and the railroads came to be regarded not as the welcome carriers of goods and persons, but as the carriers of the dreaded revolution, then the centralized State, the outgrowth of mercantilistic policies clearly became an obstacle to the economic development of the country. If the same sequence was reproduced in France by the absurd tariff policies of the Napoleonic bureaucracy after the demise of the Continental System, the intensity of the phenomenon and its negative effects were undoubtedly a good deal weaker and less damaging than was the case in Austria.

But a comparison of Austria with Russia is also illuminating, although in different respects. The effort of economic development and general reform produced by Joseph II, strong as it was, cannot be compared in magnitude and intensity to that of Peter the Great. This is as it should be as the vehemence of the spurt, the magnitude of the change, can be expected to vary with the backwardness of the country. But, in particular, the problem in Austria was not to establish a general service State, subjugating the gentry and forcing the peasantry to serve both the gentry and the State. Quite the contrary was true. The burdens of the peasantry were not

89

increased but reduced. By Joseph's edict of 1781 personal subjection of the Austrian peasantry was abolished. As a piece of what aptly was called imperial propaganda the edict spoke of the abolition of *Leibeigenschaft*, that is, slavery, which was exaggerated as the Austrian peasant was enserfed rather than enslaved. But abolition of personal subjection meant, in addition to the right to marry without consent of the seignior and the discontinuation of the hated house services by the members of the peasant's family, also, and most importantly, the right to leave the land and choose their trade freely. This was surely an approach to the problem of forming a modern labor force that was radically different from that followed in Russia. It is true that peasant obligations to the lords as attached to the land rather than to the person remained. But also in this respect, Joseph II tried a rather radical reform of compulsory commutation on a national scale. Under the terms of his edict of 10 February 1789—significantly five months before the start of the French Revolution—labor services to the seigniors were to be abolished and instead the peasant was to pay in money a fixed proportion of his gross income to the seignior and another fixed proportion to the State. This reform was never carried out for a number of weighty political and economic reasons. But the effect of the reform was perhaps not entirely nil. It left the gentry with the feeling that eventual emancipation was inevitable and as a result encouraged some of the seigniors to conclude private redemption agreements with the peasants and to replace bonded labor with freely-hired labor. Thus, at least in this respect the mercantilistic policies left no obstacles for the future.

The effect of the Petrine policies was very different. Peter, of course, was in no way the creator of serfdom in Russia. The last legal measures sealing the condition of enserfment were administered by Peter's father in the code of 1649. And yet, it is fair to say that it was Peter's policies that in a very real sense greatly increased the effectiveness of the system of serfdom. The great improvement in the efficiency of the administration, the introduction of the passport system, and, last but not least, the reform of the fiscal system by the establishment of the poll tax with its regular censuses as a form of registration of the peasantry for the first time rendered it extremely difficult for the peasants to escape from the yoke of serfdom. In the longer run, once the crisis of the last years of Peter's reign and of the few following years was overcome, the chances of a successful flight were very greatly reduced, unless indeed it be a flight from a poorer seignior to a high and mighty one who often was in a position to use his influence in order to prevent the return of the refugee to his rightful owner. In addition, as a result of Peter's policies the burdens imposed on the peasantry increased very greatly, and this not only by extending peasant services far beyond the sphere of agriculture to industry, construction, and transportation; but also within the area of agriculture. As never before, the burdens the peasants bore were regarded as work for the State.

When the great experiment was over; when after some stagnation, the country's growth was resumed at very moderate rates; when finally the Industrial Revolution in England ushered in a new era in industrial history, then it was precisely the institution of serfdom, so greatly reinforced by Peter and one of the carrying pillars of his edifice of economic development, that became the major block in the path of Russia's participation in the new industrial progress. For in the interval the nature of serfdom had profoundly changed. The reform work of the Petrine period, combined with the size of the country in area and population, effectively and long-lastingly liberated the rulers of the country from the necessity to undertake extraordinary efforts in order to maintain the military power of the country on a level sufficiently high for the purposes of expansion. For a full century after Peter's death, the Russian arms and Russian power basked in the sun of continual successes. In the south, the steppes of Novorossiya and the Crimea were wrested from the Turks, and the Russians firmly established themselves on the shores of the Black Sea. In the west, in the course of the Seven Years' War, Russian cossacks had penetrated into Berlin. The partitions of Poland meant enormous territorial expansion westward. Finally, the failure of Napoleon's invasion of Russia which in the end brought the Russian troops into the streets of Paris crowned this series of astonishing triumphs.

The modernized and stronger State no longer needed the enforced services of the gentry, and in 1762 the service obligation of the gentry was abolished by a solemn imperial manifesto. But thereby also the social function of serfdom and the rationale of its diffusion was abolished. Serfdom was no longer needed by the State and, by the same token its continuation became a problem. The return of the peasants to 'black' status, that is, to the status of State peasants owing tax payments to the State, but otherwise free would have been the natural solution. If it was considered at all in the crucial seventh decade of the eighteenth century it was never adopted. And it is not implausible to assume that it could not have been adopted. The subjugation of the peasantry, the forcible transformation of the masses of 'black peasants' into serfs or rather slaves and the concomitant transfer of 'black lands' to the *pomeshchiki*, that is, to the seigniors, had never been fully accepted by the peasants. Or rather, if the change in their personal status was, the change in the ownership of the lands was not. With the emancipation of the gentry, the traditional justification for the institution of serfdom had disappeared.

The countryside seethed with resentment and unrest until it exploded in the previously mentioned Pugachev's uprising—the Russian peasant war of 1773. I believe it is fair to say that after the uprising was quelled at the cost of a great effort, the government no longer could dare even consider the emancipation of the peasantry. The position of autocracy, strong as it was, was no longer comparable to what it used to be in Peter's time. Since Peter's death, the gentry guard had engineered two *coups d'état* which brought two empresses to the throne. The autocracy no longer operated in a social vacuum, and it needed some *points d'appui* in the society. And after Pugachev it became clearer than ever that the nobility and the gentry were the only group upon which the monarch could rely. Under these conditions, dispossessing the gentry by the abolition of serfdom would have deprived the throne of its natural ally. On the other hand, it was precisely the uprising that showed that the villages with their pent-up hatreds were powder kegs, ready to explode. A sudden relaxation of pressure might well provide the spark to ignite not an uprising but a peasant revolution in which not only the gentry but also the throne might perish. Thus it came about that far from abolishing serfdom, Catherine II increased the number of serfs enormously both by expanding it to new geographic areas and through her generous gifts of thousands and thousands of serfs. Finally, it must be noted that the term serfdom to characterize the peasants' condition in Russia, although conventional, is quite misapplied. With the strong centralized government guarding the rights of the landowners serfdom had long degenerated into outright slavery. We may continue to use the term, but we should keep in mind that it is actually a misnomer.

At any rate, whatever the reasons for its perpetuation, serfdom had become unreservedly a private service for, or slavery to, the seigniors and had lost its public law connotations. It became the decisive retarding factor in Russian economic development through most, if not all, of the nineteenth century. For the specific way in which the emancipation of the peasantry was finally carried out in 1861 preserved, even though in an attenuated form, some of the negative effects of serfdom for a considerable time after the abolition of the institution.

The interpretation of these sequences bears directly on the basic problem of Russia and Europe. And I must confess that at the present moment I still find myself in a state of some uncertainty. While I am unable now to resolve the uncertainty satisfactorily, I can at least try to clarify its nature. My usual way of looking at the Petrine experience (and applying the same idea to some earlier periods of Russian history) was to discern in it a series of sequences which I regarded as a specifically Russian pattern of economic development. To summarize the sequences briefly: 1) economic development was placed in the service of the country's military needs and was a function thereof; 2) as a result the development assumed an uneven, jerky, spurt-like character and was compressed within a relatively short period, involving 3) imposition of high, if not intolerable, burdens on the population who had the misfortune of living in those particular periods; and 4) introduction of special repressive measures, designed to force the population to bear those burdens; 5) continuation of the spurt until the decrease in military pressures and/or the exhaustion of the population led to the termination of the spurt which was followed either by stagnation, or, at any rate, by a considerable decline in the rate of growth.

I do feel that this summarizes correctly the course of the Petrine experience. The crucial problem in the preceding sequences, from the point of view of this presentation, relates to point 4: the introduction of special measures of enforcement, that is to say, the enserfment of the peasantry. It is really this point that made me feel that quantitative differences apart, here lay the peculiar qualitative specificity of the Russian pattern. While the main purpose of the Russian development was to modernize its economy, and, in fact, much of its social and political framework, that is, to bring it closer to Europe in some of its most significant respects, it was by the force of the selfsame development that Russia was being forced in other, no less significant respects, away from Europe, towards the despotisms of the Orient with their service states, which involved enslavement of the population by the State.

I do not feel that there is anything wrong *per se* with this presentation. It is a significant fact that as serfdom was on the wane in the west of Europe it was greatly increasing in Russia. If human freedom is one criterion of civilization, then, Russia was becoming less civilized as—*and because*—it was aspiring to move closer to Europe, or, as Hjärne would say, to enter the community of European civilization. As I shall try to explain presently, I have tended to view the decisive 'Europeanization' of Russian economy as pertaining to a much later period— the last three decades before the outbreak of World War I. And yet, I have begun to wonder whether even the Petrine period and the policies of Russian mercantilism could not be regarded as an integral part of a general European experience, and this in a sense that goes a good deal beyond the fact that the Russian experience can be subsumed under a general European concept of mercantilism and that actually looking into the Russian mirror has helped us to develop such a concept. What I am referring to now is the problem of the deviations in the individual countries and the chance of systematizing these deviations into a general pattern. The hypothesis then is as follows: everywhere mercantilism in promoting economic development was creating obstacles to the perpetuation of development, and the magnitude of these obstacles varied in a comprehensible fashion with the backwardness of the country. It could then be argued that it was the very weakness of such obstacles in the most advanced countries that, perhaps paradoxically, rendered possible there a destructive onslaught upon mercantilism, or, at

95

any rate, upon what was re-defined and re-constructed as mercantilism for the purposes of that onslaught.

I am offering this proposition with all the appropriate diffidence. For what is needed now is an effort in research designed to find out whether a more or less regular pattern of such obstacles, varying from country to country in magnitude and intensity and resulting in something approaching a fair *continuum* (in the botanical rather than mathematical sense of the word), can actually be ascertained. The results of such research, of course, cannot be anticipated. But, I believe, it is fairly clear that should such a meaningful pattern be discoverable, its unity would depend more on formal than substantive criteria. In other words, there will still remain some room for viewing the Russian mercantilistic experience as having had peculiar, that is to say, downright un-European substantive features. For what is likely to be involved is not just the aggregate magnitude and intensity of the obstacles created, but also their very nature.

4

In the preceding lecture I have tried to show in what way Russian economic history can help us in formulating a general concept of mercantilism; beyond that I have also intimated in a tentative fashion how the legacy of mercantilistic policies—that is, their long-term effects upon economic development—may become comprehensible as a graduated pattern, once the Russian experience is seen as an integral part of a general European pattern.

In this last lecture I planned to deal with a problem that represents a natural continuation of our discussion of mercantilism; that is, to demonstrate how the phenomenon of Russian industrialization in the three decades or so before the outbreak of World War I can be found illuminating for the history of modern industrial development in Europe in the eighteenth and nineteenth centuries. This is still my purpose, except that I could not help making this lecture much more polemical than had been my original intention, and also inserting within its purview a discussion of Soviet industrial history. Let me explain what caused me to change my plans.

As I was preparing this lecture, I stumbled across the fine Festschrift which Charles Feinstein had edited in honor of Maurice Dobb.[1] This volume contains an essay by E. H. Carr in which he raises a number of severe, if not vicious, objections to my treatment of the industrial development of Europe in the nineteenth century.[2] Not every criticism calls for a reply. But a critique which distorts and perverts the nature of a historical interpretation and, in addition, poses some general methodological questions should not go unanswered; least of all

97

in a lecture given at Cambridge, seeing that the criticism was produced by a Fellow of Trinity College in a volume edited by a Fellow of Clare College in honor of a Fellow of Trinity College. The confusion that has been created at Cambridge must be clarified at Cambridge.

A comprehensive view of my approach was presented in two volumes of essays to which some references were made in the preceding lectures.[3] Before dealing with Professor Carr's criticism, I must recall, with all suitable brevity, the essential features of my approach.

The units of observation are the individual countries of Europe. Naturally, this is not the only possible way of looking at industrial history. Its usefulness must depend on the economic significance of political boundaries which clearly varied from period to period. Moreover, at any time, it can be argued that concentrating on a large trading area, as Rostow once suggested, even though he failed to live up to his own suggestion, or even on civilization, as Toynbee has urged with similar results, may be quite justifiable. On the other hand, since industrialization is never distributed evenly over the face of the country, also study of the industrial region or regions within the country can be worth undertaking. The validity of the regional approach no doubt will vary inversely with the mobility of factors and the distribution of demand within the country, that is to say, with the degree to which non-industrial regions support and promote the process of industrialization. At any rate, all those decisions in accordance with an ancient prescription must be recognized and judged by their fruits. What I am trying to display here is a fruit basket from the little orchard of my approach.

The basic proposition is that within each of the individual countries in Europe certain specific features of the industrialization process depended on the level of relative backwardness of the countries concerned on the eve of the period of great accelerations in their industrial

98

growth. What was found to vary in direct relation to the degree of backwardness were:

1) the speed of industrial growth;

2) the stress on bigness of plant and enterprise;

3) the composition of the nascent output, that is, the degree to which 'heavy' industries were favored;

4) the reliance on technological borrowing and perhaps financial assistance from abroad;

5) the pressure on the levels of consumption;

6) the passive role of agriculture;

7) the role of banks and State budgets;

8) the virulence of ideologies, under the auspices of which the industrialization proceeded.

Implied in this proposition is the belief that the 'degree of backwardness' is an operational concept in the sense that it can be determined with a degree of accuracy that is sufficient for the purposes of the approach. In view of the confusion Professor Carr has created (as will be shown presently), it is important to stress that the degree of backwardness must be determined *independently* from any of the features of the process of industrialization as listed in the preceding. It so happens that by and large it makes little difference whether we select as our yardstick of backwardness the size of per capita income or the network of communications existing in the country, or certain qualities of its population, such as the degree of literacy. While these yardsticks are not additive, use of any one of them would result in the same ordering of the individual countries with regard to the degree of backwardness, and even though a cardinal determination would be desirable, an ordinal determination is perfectly sufficient in this context.

Now, an essential element of the approach is my treatment of the concept of prerequisites of industrial development, and a few words must be said about it. The general tendency in literature has been not only to emphasize the importance of prerequisites, but to operate

99

with a very general, one might say, absolute or dogmatic concept of prerequisites or preconditions. This was already fairly clear in the traditional stage schemes which were in vogue with the representatives of the German historical school and which found a good deal of imitation and elaboration in Anglo-American literature. While there were differences among the individual scholars, on the whole it is correct to say that they all regarded each stage as a necessary precondition for the next stage. This is particularly clear in the work of the most recent stage schemer, Walt Rostow, who expressly builds a 'stage of preconditions' as a separate floor into his five-story edifice of economic development. And Rostow takes his concept of prerequisites seriously indeed. He speaks of necessary and sufficient preconditions, just as in a logical definition there are necessary and sufficient conditions.[4]

A good example of what is meant are agrarian reforms. They are regarded as a necessary prerequisite of industrialization. Without such reforms, it is said, an industrialization in Europe could not begin at all. Only if the peasants were freed from the trammels of an institutional framework which limited their mobility could industry receive the labor it needed. Only a flourishing peasant agriculture emerging from a properly conceived and correctly administered agrarian reform could constitute a large and growing market for industrial goods and sustain the demand for them. Only a so reformed agriculture could supply the growing industry with foodstuffs and, in less developed countries also, engage in exports of agricultural produce and thereby insert a rather fixed item into the balance of payments, so as to provide foreign exchange for imports of machinery and for the service of industrialization loans. All these relationships appear so logical, so compelling that one is indeed tempted to regard them in the light of historical necessity and to draw the conclusion that in cases where these prerequisites were lacking no industrialization could take place.

100

The only difficulty is that these beautiful exercises in logic have been defeated by history. They are not very consistent with crude empiricism, and are damaged seriously when confronted with the relevant facts as we know them.

I shall return to the agrarian problem presently, but first let us consider even more briefly the problem of financing, that is, of providing capital, in the sense of capital disposition, to industry. Let us for this purpose look at the extremely interesting attempt by Karl Marx to view what he called original accumulation of capital as a precondition to modern industrialization.[5] Marx's presentation is somewhat elliptical, but what he meant in using the concept no doubt was something like this: original accumulation means storing up of wealth from previous national incomes—through very long periods—which accumulation at a favorable moment—when the hour of industrialization has struck—can be converted into claims against current national income, so that entrepreneurs can get the means to compete labor and materials away from consumption and old firms. In this way they can initiate processes of forced savings which enable them to carry out the needed investment projects and acquire capital in the real sense of the term. Original accumulation, too, has been regarded as a necessary precondition of the industrialization, and until very recently Soviet economic historians kept looking, looking everywhere, in every country where any industrial development had taken place, for such original accumulation. Again we should have to conclude that where there was no original accumulation, no industrialization could take place.

Let us cast, however, a quick glance upon three countries which we pare out as paradigms from the complex of industrializations: England, Germany, and Russia; and let us ask how were capital dispositions essentially obtained in those three countries. We should admit, I think, that something in the nature of original accumulation indeed played an important role in England; although we should be wary in regarding it as the sole source. When it comes to Germany it would be much more difficult, in fact impossible, to assign great significance to original accumulation. The role of the strategic factor in that country was surely played by the investment bank. The investment bank, which so happily combined the functions of a commercial bank with those of financing industrial enterprises, was a creative innovation, perhaps the greatest organizational innovation in the economic history of the century. This was an activity, which, like most innovations, was little understood and not little resisted by the contemporaries, including the economists, who regarded the investment banks with distrust and suspicion, considered them unsound, and issued dark prophesies about the inevitability of impending catastrophes. And if we move on farther eastward into Russia, we see that the same function in the great upswing of the 1890s was exercised by the State, that is to say, the State budget which used the power of the State to collect, through taxation, funds from the population and pass them on to industrial entrepreneurs. Again industrialization occurred, even though a so-called necessary prerequisite was missing.

At this point in the development of my approach I felt that a choice had to be made. I could have abandoned the concept of prerequisites altogether, since it had fared so poorly when confronted with historical reality in crucially significant areas. But this would not have been a fruitful decision. For the concept of prerequisites of industrial development can serve us in good stead once we have divested it of its absolute character. If we return for a moment to the problem of financing industrial development, as previously discussed, then we may say indeed that in England original accumulation could be usefully regarded as a prerequisite for industrialization.

But then we may say that the German investment bank was a substitute for the missing or inadequately available prerequisite. In Russia, where for many reasons a credit system could not function in the early stages of industrialization, the budget was a substitute for both the missing prerequisite and the yet inapplicable German substitution. Once we view the industrial development of Europe in this fashion, it appears indeed as a unity, but not as the simplicist, homogeneous unity, as it appeared to stage theorists from Friedrich List to Walt Rostow, but as a complex, graduated unity where the degree of backwardness of the individual areas is the dominant factor determining the nature of the substitutions that have taken place.

I am saying this deliberately in this generalized fashion, because capital disposition is only one of the very many examples of an orderly pattern of substitutions that could be cited. Let us have another brief glance at a specific agrarian reform. In 1861, serfdom was abolished in Russia. Without going into any details, let me just say that in consequence of the way in which the reform had been carried out, the peasants, oppressed by inadequate holdings and high redemption payments, could neither develop rising demand for industrial goods nor increase substantially the productivity of agriculture; at the same time, the village commune acted as a high barrier against flight from the land, and thus tended to impede the formation of the industrial labor force. And yet, the industrialization took place. How then was it achieved? Essentially through a number of specific substitutions. The demand of the peasants was substituted for by the demand of the State for capital goods. The inadequate labor supply was substituted for by introduction of modern labor-saving technology. The insufficient increases in productivity in agriculture were substituted for by pressure on the income levels of the peasantry. And the cases of substitutions of this kind were not confined to the effects of the

103

conditions of agriculture. They extended to the whole area of the industrial economy, the importation of technology and qualified personnel from abroad being a substitute for the missing prerequisite of indigenous knowledge and deficiency in educational background. Just as to some extent both the exaggerated size of plants and the role of government bureaucracy substituted for the inadequate supply of entrepreneurs.

Geographically seen, that is to say, spatially speaking, all these substitutions, their numbers and intensity can be explained in terms of the rising degree of backwardness of the areas concerned. To do so, gives us first of all an opportunity to bring some order into the apparent chaos, to establish, that is, a morphology or typology of the development. But the approach yields more enlightenment than just a spatial ordering of events. As we follow the course of the industrial spurt over time, we see how under the impact of diminishing backwardness also the pattern of substitutions begins to change and substitutions characteristic of a high degree of backwardness begin to be replaced by substitutions that have been used in areas of medium backwardness. In this fashion, temporally seen, the original morphology becomes more complex, is given a causal twist, and its organizing principle of the degree of backwardness becomes then a causal principle, explaining for us the nature of the processes of industrial change.

Based on the foregoing, I have hazarded the following generalization: the more advanced a country, the richer is its pre-industrial history and the simpler is its industrial history. But the more backward a country, the more barren appears its pre-industrial landscape and the more complex and exciting its industrial history precisely because it is shot through with substitutions of all kinds.

This then is, stripped of details, my picture of European industrialization. Let us see now how it appears in the crooked mirror of Professor Carr's presentation. Professor Carr has chosen to use my approach as a springboard for his leap into 'Some Random Reflections on Soviet Industrialization'. He does pick up at random what I have said about use of different institutional elements varying with the degree of backwardness, and then goes on to say that one of my favorite concepts is substitution with its 'implication of the inferior and factitious' (*op. cit.* p. 272). He then proceeds to accuse me of some romantic nostalgia for the British type of industrialization, declares that 'nostalgia for the past seldom makes good history', and upbraids me because in a 'work which professes to place economic backwardness in historical perspective', I have not taken a sufficiently critical look at that historical perspective (pp. 272-4). Thus I am charged with an emotional attachment to England's Industrial Revolution and in addition with being unhistorical.

Before I deal with the substance of Professor Carr's criticism let me say that I do not find it surprising to see him make these points. This is only another instance of the technique he displayed so prominently in his well-known G. M. Trevelyan Lectures.[6] Whenever he did not like an historian, he charged him with being emotional and unhistorical. Now I have not the slightest notion what emotions rage in Professor Carr's breast, nor could I care less. I know from reading those lectures that Professor Carr has a little set of propositions of charming simplicity which he offers at a low price as a sociology or psychology of historical writings. He is interested in unavowed and unconscious motivations. I have no way of exploring my subconsciousness, and it is entirely possible that I write as I write because at the crucial age of four I was madly in love with a grand-aunt of mine, or because of my castration complex, or for whatever other reason Professor Carr's shallow depth psychology or poor man's sociology might suggest; quite apart from the possibility that my wet nurse, in an unguarded moment, may have dropped me on my head. The fact is that I am not conscious of any nostalgic feelings about eighteenth- or nineteenth-century England, nor about anything else for that matter.[7] It is true that I am not particularly elated about the present, even though I realize that the acquisitive society in the West has improved considerably over my lifetime, and even the State in the east of Europe, that very acquisitive and inquisitive—or rather inquisitorial—State, is no longer quite as horrible as it used to be. But my point is that those things are of interest only if Professor Carr intends to write my biography or to do me the honor of working my little approach into a big canvas, painted with his sociological brushes, on the condition of economic history in the United States. I submit, however, that all this stuff is exquisitely irrelevant in judging the truth content of my approach, by which I mean the plausibility of my interpretations of historical reality; that is to say, the degree to which they satisfy a reasonable man's sense of reasoned adequacy.

And as far as the other charge of being unhistorical goes, let me say that I am quite tired of people who go around telling me what history is and what it is not. At present, the discipline of economic history in the United States is passing through a rather revolutionary stage. Thanks to the application of economic analysis and generous use of quantitative tools of research new questions are being addressed to the material and new and exciting answers are obtained. This is far and away the best thing that has happened to the discipline in generations. But conventional economic historians keep telling us that this is dehumanization of history and consequently not history at all. In my view, any scholarly treatment of past events and sequences of events is history. It may be, as Thomas Hardy used to say, 'rattling good history' or shockingly poor history, but history it will be; and authoritarian dictation by men who like to couch their highly subjective preferences and biases in academic garbs and to tell us in advance what our findings must be is clearly incompatible with the very essence of scholarship.

Turning now to the substance of Professor Carr's criticism, let me first point to his complete misunderstanding of my concept of substitutions for missing prerequisites. Far from regarding them as 'inferior or factitious', I have always seen them in the nature of creative innovations. Professor Carr, who likes to speak of lessons from history, should have recognized that emphasizing the role of substitutions in industrial history offers a much more optimistic view of the chances for industrial development of currently undeveloped or underdeveloped countries. As previously said, it was the traditional view that industrialization cannot take place unless a number of 'necessary prerequisites' have been created. In the case of Russia, for instance, quite reputable writers used to argue not only that industrialization required the prerequisite of a broad internal market, not only that a large bourgeoisie must first come into being, but that even radical changes in the national character of the Russian people were necessary before industrial development could begin. This is a profoundly pessimistic view of industrial history. There is, of course, in principle nothing wrong with a pessimistic view if it is borne out by the facts. But in this case it was not. I happen to have somewhat less confidence than Professor Carr in our ability to draw lessons from history. My primary objective is to understand the past, and for this, I believe, the concept of substitutions—which incidentally, as every economist knows, even though Professor Carr does not, is in itself a perfectly neutral term with no derogatory connotations—performs very useful service. It offers us some predictive possibilities—predictive in the technical, historical sense. This means that once a basic hypothesis relating a pattern of substitutions in their nature and intensity to the degree of economic backwardness has been formulated, it becomes possible, when embarking on research in a new area, to determine the degree of backwardness of that area and then establish a set of expectations with regard to the substitutions that one is likely to find. In other words, one knows what to look for, and this is of inestimable value in research.

Professor Carr says: 'Though Gerschenkron disclaims any intention of setting up a norm of industrialization, the application of a criterion of backwardness inevitably leads to this result' (*ibid.*). The inevitability and the result are in Professor Carr's imagination. To some extent, the concept of substitutions may have been actually alive in the minds of the contemporaries; of those that is, who were the agents of the development in backward countries. But it need not have been. Men may have been quite ignorant of the history of more advanced countries. They may have simply groped for and found effective solutions to the pressing problems of their time. In another sense, therefore, the concept of substitutions may be considered simply as a construct that just helps to understand the process of industrialization and to conceive Europe in this regard as a graduated unit. In principle, it would have been possible to start with Russia and then see the investment bank in central Europe as a substitution for the State budget in Russia, and the original accumulation in turn as a substitute for the investment bank. This would not have been a very useful way of looking at things. Not because the last vestiges of the concept of prerequisites would be lost in the process, but for very good empirical reasons. For some of the substitutions, in a very important fashion, implied the existence of advanced countries.

This is another way of saying that history moves forward and not backward. And yet for some limited purposes even the view of history *à rebours*—in the reverse gear—may be unexceptionable.[8]

Thus, there is no intention to regard England as the

norm or the 'model'. England, in my scheme of things, is not the 'model' in Professor Carr's sense; it is an integral part of the model which I have tried to present. It is not the inevitable result of my construct, but a fact of industrial history of Europe that, as backwardness was diminishing by virtue of industrialization, backward countries tended, in several important respects, to move closer to more advanced countries. What I have done is to specify those respects, as I found them in the actual process of industrialization. It is the empirical course of events that lends crucial support to my supposition that the patterns of substitution are a function of the degree of backwardness of a country, because they tended to change in a comprehensible, predictable way with changes in the degree of backwardness. This was the case in Europe during the period before 1914 with which alone I was concerned. And I was careful to point out that in other periods and in other conditions this process of assimilation may not occur. In saying this, I had particularly the Soviet experience in mind, about which something more will be said presently. But as far as the period before 1914 goes, even Professor Carr is forced to admit, even though reluctantly, that 'it is probably'— probably!—'correct that between 1906 and 1914 Russian industrialization came nearer than at any other time to the pattern of industrialization of Western countries' (p. 276). This, one should have thought, is the recantation of the critic.

But Professor Carr has still another argument up his sleeve. For he continues the admission just quoted by saying; 'But this is only half the story' (*ibid.*), and he proceeds to argue that Russian industrialization was not backward because in the process much more advanced methods were used than had been the case in more advanced countries. The trouble with this argument is that the 'other half of the story' is not Professor Carr's, but very much my own, and I must protest against infringement of my property rights. In my studies of industrialization in conditions of backwardness, I went to considerable length to stress what I called the advantages of backwardness, that is to say, the advantages of the latecomers. The most important of these advantages was precisely the possibility of application of more efficient modern technology and, concomitantly, of fuller utilization of economies of scale. I also tried to explain why the traditional view of factor proportions in backward countries was inadequate, and that in reality factor proportions, within broad limits, favored rather than impeded introduction of labor-saving technology. Such technology was precisely a substitute for the shortcomings of the labor force, both quantitative and qualitative. To try to confound my approach by something that is an integral part thereof is curious, to say the least. The purpose of this strange exercise apparently is to show that Soviet Russia was not a backward country. Unfortunately, the debating trick involved in shifting the meaning of backwardness from a description of the condition of the country on the eve of its industrialization to the way in which this condition is being improved, is what the medieval doctors used to call a *quaternio terminorum*, in other words a logical fallacy. And it is no more pleasant to see Professor Carr claim that I regarded a country as backward because the State and not private entrepreneurs were the moving force of industrialization. What I have said is exactly the opposite: the State played its role because the country was backward. Had I said what Professor Carr imputes to me, I should have been indeed guilty of circular reasoning, but my critic fails to notice this not very subtle point. In my book neither juggling terms nor perversion of meaning and causal nexus is considered the very best show of scholarship. In Henri Monnier's wonderful classic, *Les Mémoires de Joseph Prudhomme*,[9] there appears a painter sitting on the embankment of the Seine and offering to paint

portraits of the passers-by. He has a price list attached
to his easel. It reads:

> *Ressemblance Parfaite*—25 francs
> *Demi-Ressemblance*   —15 francs
> *Air de Famille*   —5 francs

I doubt that Professor Carr's portrayal of my approach,
in which even the family looks are blurred, would rate 5
francs, particularly of the purchasing power of the 1850s.

While the foregoing should make clear the misleading
and unguarded nature of Professor Carr's criticism, it
does not reveal its purpose. The attack upon my approach
was meant to bolster Professor Carr's defense of Soviet
industrialization. This, I believe, betrays a further fatal
misunderstanding of my interpretation and raises, in
addition to substantive issues, a fundamental methodological problem with regard to the limits of an historical
interpretation.

Professor Carr has attempted to view the Soviet industrialization as a natural continuation of the general
pattern of industrializations from the Industrial Revolution in England onward. The crucial passage must be
cited *in extenso*:

'When industrialization began in Great Britain in the
middle of the eighteenth century, manufacture was
still *manu*facture. The individual entrepreneur working
with a dozen or a score of "hands" was the typical unit
of production; tools and machines were of the simplest
kind; the capital investment required to float such
enterprises was very small. It may be true that the
British economy was somewhat more advanced—in
the sense of having larger resources in capital and skill
—when it embarked on industrialization—than the
continental and Russian economies of a later date
when they started on the same course. But the much
more significant fact is that, in the conditions of the

latter part of the eighteenth century, far smaller capital resources and less technical knowhow were needed to set the process of industrialization in motion. The problem of capital accumulation, which bedeviled the latter type of industrialization, arose only in the second stage of British industrialization, when internal resources had multiplied sufficiently to cope with it. When continental Europe embarked on industrialization in the middle of the nineteenth century, the essential conditions had changed. Railway construction dominated the process. Large units of production, heavy and complicated machines and large investments of capital were the order of the day. When Russia followed the same path fifty years later, technology had made further advances, and then developments were further intensified. Hence the progression from the primitive British model of industrialization by the private entrepreneur through the more advanced continental model of financing and control by the banks to the still more advanced Russian model of financing and control by the State, already discernible in the Russian industrialization of the eighteen-nineties.

The conclusion I should like to draw is that Soviet industrialization is neither a unique phenomenon, nor a deviation from an established and accepted model, but an important stage in a process of development which began two centuries ago and still looks to have a long history before it. The specific feature of Soviet industrialization is its association with a planned economy. . . .'[10]

The reader will understand that I am unable to disagree entirely with the first long paragraph of this quotation. For it contains, in faithful reproduction, some elements of my approach to the industrial development of Europe. As I was describing the role of the banks in areas of medium backwardness and the role of the State in areas of still greater backwardness, I duly noted that

112

evolution of technology and changing composition of industrial output induced growing capital-output ratios and made for increases in the optimal size of plant. This naturally rendered more arduous the task of providing the requisite capital dispositions.

And yet, the paragraph which on the face of it seems to be a summary of my approach, is hardly more than a caricature thereof. For what is wrong with that paragraph is not what is said, but what is being suppressed. And this happens to be the essential features of my interpretation. First of all, if rising capital-output ratios are to tell the whole story, how are we to explain the decline in the importance of the banks in Germany and the considerable withdrawal of the State from industrial promotion in Russia after 1900? Surely, the reasons cannot lie in any fall in capital-output ratios and decrease in the optimal size of plant. In fact, the very contrary is known to have been the case. What Professor Carr has appropriated from my approach is thus incapable of explaining crucial phases in the process of industrialization.

Nor can one take seriously the view that differences in that process are simply a function of the passage of time and of the technological evolution that occurred within it. The implication of Professor Carr's presentation is that if the great spurt of industrialization in imperial Russia had occurred several decades earlier, it would have proceeded in exact conformity with the industrialization in Germany. Or, to put it differently, why were there decisive differences between the process of industrialization in Russia and in Italy, even though the great spurts in the two countries occurred at about the same time? In other words, what Professor Carr has excised from my approach is its carrying pillar; that is to say, the varying degrees of backwardness of the countries concerned.

The problem of providing capital dispositions for industry was so serious in backward countries not just because

113

of rising capital-output ratios. Provision of capital was inhibited by the very backwardness of the countries concerned. And the problem was further and crucially aggravated by the fact that industrialization in conditions of backwardness could occur only in the form of a big push, thus utilizing the advantages of what Eric Dahmén called 'development blocs',[11] determined, on the supply side, by indivisibilities and particularly by complementarities. Hence the high rates of growth of industrial output in the great spurts in backward countries, and hence the great pressure on the inadequate capital resources.

But industrialization in its further course provided its own cure against capital scarcities. As economic backwardness was being diminished by successful industrialization, capital dispositions grew more and more abundant. The one trouble with Professor Carr's unilinear view of development—so reminiscent of the stage schemers, old and new—is that it offers no explanation of the highly-significant developments that took place in Germany and Russia before 1914. And as far as Soviet Russia is concerned, the incongruity of using capital-output ratios as the main explanatory factor in Soviet economic history should be quite patent. Surely, the discrepancy between that causal factor and its alleged effects in terms of the enormous phenomenon of Soviet industrialization, encased in its mighty political framework, is much too wide for plausibility and credibility.

Let me, therefore, try to explain how Soviet industrial history relates to my approach and why I believe that it contains crucial elements that render difficult, if not impossible, its incorporation within the confines of that approach. There is no doubt that the Soviet experience displays, if anything, in an exaggerated form the peculiar features of industrialization in conditions of backwardness. First of all, a rate of growth of industrial output was achieved which, although much lower than the claims made, was a good deal higher than the rate attained in the 1890s. The stress on heavy industry, as we observed it in Soviet Russian history, was altogether unprecedented in the history of any other backward country, including the Russian experience of the 1890s when Russia was economically much less advanced than it became in the later part of the twenties, on the eve of the First Five Year Plan. And obviously, the burdens imposed on the population, the war apart, far exceeded the very great sacrifices that the population had been called upon to make in the 1890s. Equally unprecedented was the extent of technological borrowings from abroad in the period of the First Five Year Plan, when the volume of foreign trade reached its highest level ever, while goods not directly connected with economic development were severely excluded from Russian imports. The same was true of the size of plant and enterprise. For some time the very idea that from a certain point on there might be some disadvantages to bigness was decried as a bourgeois prejudice, until eventually, under the pressure of a threatened war and the growing demonstration of inefficiencies, the attitude changed and construction of plants of excessive size began to be described as gigantomania and regarded as evidence of sinister plots against the State. And as far as the institutional framework of industrialization is concerned, the role of the State was, of course, equally unprecedented in being the sole organizer and carrier of industrial development.

Finally, as previously mentioned, in the European pattern also the intensity of the industrialization ideology used to vary with the degree of backwardness. In no other country, be it Saint-Simonism in France, or nationalism in Germany, or Marxism in Russia of the 1890s, was ideology playing a comparably large part. The highly hybrid ideological concoction that went under the misnomer of Marxism was continually readjusted to endow any act of the industrialization policy with a Scripture-like sanction, and so to blur and to disguise the actual

115

motivations and aims of that policy. Thus, in an economically ignorant and untenable, but politically very meaningful fashion, the more rapid growth of output of producers' goods as against output of consumers' goods was solemnly declared to be an absolute condition for industrial growth and defended with an irrelevant reference to Marx's theory of the market.[12]

To repeat, all the individual features of what I have described as a pattern of European industrialization in conditions of very great backwardness were not only present, but present with a vengeance. If one wanted to conceive of planning as a substitution for the market—as a specific technique, that is, in conditions of backwardness—there is no doubt that a multitude of ingenious and creative innovations have been introduced in the process, and had been always inherent in the very concept of substitution.

And yet, this is only one aspect of the Soviet pattern of development. For it has displayed specific aspects which do not fit into the European pattern. The very virulence, the extreme form of which those features of industrialization assumed since the First Five Year Plan, was hardly consonant with the state of backwardness in which the country found itself when at the end of the NEP period it had again reached and somewhat exceeded the levels of 1914. This in itself might suggest that something else was involved in the Soviet pattern. And, indeed, if the European pattern could be viewed as essentially an economic pattern, only somewhat accentuated by military considerations, in Russia the threat of war, the fear of what was known in Russia as 'capitalist encirclement' no doubt played an incomparably larger part in initiating the period of Soviet super-industrialization.

But there was also something else and more important in the Soviet pattern that was at variance with the European experience. And that was the introduction of

116

special institutional arrangements designed to force the population to accept and to bear the enormous burdens that were imposed on it. I am referring, of course, to the 'revolution from above', as Stalin termed it, using an apt phrase, appropriately first coined by a chief of Nicholas I's secret police. The collectivization of agriculture, the placing of the majority of Russian population into the strait-jacket of collective farms not only signified the end and the reversal of the agrarian revolution in Russia. Functionally, the collectivization performed the same function as the serfdom in the Petrine period, as indeed was the re-establishment in Soviet Russia of the Petrine 'service state'. Once more, in the history of the country the attempt to modernize it, to bring it technologically and in the levels of output closer to the West, was accompanied by the country's being thrown in some regards away from the West towards the pattern of the ancient Oriental despotisms. It is with reference to this feature of Soviet industrialization that I wrote of return to patterns that before World War I seemed to belong to a long bygone period. In this sense, the Soviet experience displays clear elements of Russian mercantilism, and by the same token, of mercantilism in general; and any talk about that experience representing the last word of human progress, the main thesis and conclusion of Professor Carr's 'Random Reflections', must perforce try to gloss over this crucial aspect of Soviet economic development.

But this is not the end of the story. For along with resemblances with Russian mercantilism, there is also a basic difference. Whatever the opposition of the population against Peter the Great, he was—as were the other mercantilist rulers in Europe—a legitimate monarch. As I have mentioned in my second lecture, in order to oppose him legends denying his legitimacy had to be invented. By contrast, the Soviet dictatorship, as all modern dictatorships, was confronted with the perennial problem to establish a justification, a *raison d'être* for its existence. A dictatorship deprived of either the divine sanction and the ancientness of its tradition which were successfully claimed by the monarchy or the active and effective consent of the governed upon which democracy rests, is inherently unstable in the sense of being under steady pressure to vindicate itself, that is to say, to assure and re-assure the stability conditions of its power. I have listed those conditions elsewhere as follows:[13]

1) maintenance of a permanent condition of stress and strain

a) by the existence or creation of enemies, both internal and external

b) by imposing upon the population gigantic tasks that exert strong pressures upon its standard of well-being, or, at least, greatly retard improvements in those standards;

2) incessant exercise of dictatorial power;

3) creation of an image of the dictator as incarnation of supreme wisdom and indomitable will power;

4) reference to an allegedly unchanged and unchangeable value system, by which the actions of the dictatorship are justified;

5) proscription of any deviating values and beliefs coupled with threats and acts of repression.

These stability conditions constitute, I believe, a fair presentation of Soviet policy during the Stalin era. In a sense, they are still related to the mercantilistic period because they are essentially based on power and the urge to maintain and to increase the power of the regime. But the fundamental internal instability introduces altogether new elements into the picture. It is true that unlike the Petrine experience, the Soviet spurt of growth, conducted under modern conditions, cannot end in a period of stagnation. The flexibility of the modern economy is such that it allows of a relatively easy readjustment involving a shift from producers' goods to consumers' goods, while leaving enough room for a reduced but still fair rate of growth. But this similarity with the general European pattern of industrialization is counteracted by the self-perpetuating urges of the dictatorship. The primacy of the political factor clearly distinguishes the Soviet industrialization from the general European pattern of industrialization in conditions of varying backwardness. The latter could be interpreted essentially in economic terms with the political factor playing an additional limited role. In the Soviet experience it is the political factor that dominates the situation, and the staggering human cost of Soviet experience cannot be seen in merely economic terms.

It is true, as said before, that the burdens imposed on the population by individual industrializations tended on the whole to vary directly with the degree of backwardness of the areas concerned; and Professor Carr cannot really mean it, when he is willing to congratulate 'other countries on having been lucky enough as latecomers to avoid some of the worst evils of British industrial revolution'.[14] For he quickly changes his tune and refuses to contest 'the view that Soviet industrialization was responsible for the death of more people, or made people more unhappy, or raised standards of living more slowly, than the British industrialization'.[15] To try to do so would be an unrewarding enterprise indeed. Instead, he brushes the point aside by declaring that such considerations 'do not lead anywhere', and he remains quite philosophical on the problem of human cost by arguing in his lectures on *What is History?*[16] that, after all, any beneficial innovation from the printing press to the automobile was abused and was and is costly in terms of human happiness. Much as I disagree with Professor Carr, I do not regard his particular abuse of the printing press comparable in its negative effects to what was experienced by a single victim of Stalin's rule. And again I do not admire the lightness of touch with which he disposes

119

of the problem of Soviet dictatorship by describing it as an escape from the 'intolerable Hobbesian state of nature'.[17] For the state of Soviet affairs which could be fairly described in Horatio's words as characterized by 'carnal, bloody, and unnatural acts' was indeed 'unnatural', but hardly less tolerable. And as one reads the literature that has recently come out of Soviet Russia describing life under Stalin, one is not sure how un-Hobbesian was a situation in which indeed the attitude of *homo homini lupus* seemed to prevail.

But the problem which I am discussing is not a moral one. It is a problem of historical interpretation: to wit, the relation of the Soviet experience to the general pattern of European industrialization. The human cost bears on the problem only because it underlines with particular clarity the political nature of that experience. It was a distinguishing feature of European industrializations in the nineteenth century that, whatever the degree of backwardness of the country concerned, they allowed a smooth transition from the great spurts of growth to the post-spurt periods. It is a peculiarity of Soviet industrialization that the political regime of the country must be considered as the main obstacle to such a transition.

For a decade and a half Soviet Russia has been in the throes of a succession crisis. In its course, some of the stability conditions of dictatorial power exercise have been considerably weakened. No one can predict what the future will bring: a decay and disintegration of dictatorial power, its complete re-assertion, or continued lingering in the present grey twilight that followed upon the Stalinist night. These uncertainties are clearly reflected in the back and forth of economic policies; in the continual waverings between centralization and decentralization, which, too, are essentially politically motivated.

The problem, of course, is not the continued existence of planning, whose manifold inefficiencies, incidentally, may have contributed in the past to increases in capital-output ratios, as Professor Carr might have noted but did not. The problem rather is a change in the nature and in goals of planning. Some limited progress has been made in the direction in recent years. But it has been held in check by the vital interests of the dictatorship. Changes in the nature of planning are at variance with the need of the dictatorship to interfere incessantly and arbitrarily with the operation of economic units, such interference being perhaps the most important stability condition of the dictatorship. The regime which initiated and carried through the greatest spurt in the industrial history of the country is at present an obstacle, not primarily perhaps to a continuation of growth (although the inefficiencies implied in central management of the huge economic establishment are great indeed), but to the utilization of the fruits of growth by the population.

It is, of course, possible that in the end the force of diminished backwardness will assert itself also in the Soviet Union. But what has been happening there since the death of Stalin is at best a slow and uncertain movement away from what came to be regarded as the normalcy of the Soviet economic system; a movement that can be reversed at any time.

At any rate, let me repeat that observing the whole process of Soviet industrialization with its Petrine-like subjugation of the peasantry and the specific self-perpetuating force of an inherently unstable dictatorship, it is difficult to escape the conclusion that the Soviet experience lies outside the sphere of the last century's European industrializations and displays some affinity with Russian economic policies of a much more remote past.

Thus, there is a great deal more to the peculiarities of Soviet industrialization than Professor Carr's changes over time in capital-output ratios. I happen to be an economic historian. Professor Carr is not. I am, therefore, sensible of the irony implied in an economist's having to explain to a political historian that any interpretation of Soviet industrialization which ignores the primacy of the political factor in Soviet history must be inadequate and misleading.

I must return now to the main problem of these lectures, that is, Russia's position *vis-à-vis* Europe and the illumination that can be derived from Russian industrial experience for the industrial history of the West. As far as the first point is concerned, it has been touched upon in the excursus into Professor Carr's ill-starred strictures, and only a few remarks remain to be made. As we look at the great spurt of industrialization in imperial Russia during the roughly three decades from 1885 on, it is necessary to divide the period into two parts: the first, from 1885 to the end of the century, and the second (leaving aside the turbulent intermission of depression, war, and revolution), from 1906 to 1914. I have tended to regard the first sub-period as containing some, though not all, features of what with some reservations I have called the specific Russian pattern of economic development. Russia's defeat, although diplomatic and not military, after the Russo-Turkish war and the recognition, once more forced upon Russian statesmen, that the country was still in no position to face a Western military power were certainly a major motivation in launching the great spurt of Russian industrialization. Furthermore, the great burdens imposed on the majority of the population resulted, by the end of the century, in a situation where the forces and the patience of the population were exhausted. The Revolution of 1905 and the great peasant unrest which preceded it and culminated in that year must be seen to have been caused, significantly and perhaps primarily, by the great and costly industrial effort of the 1890s.

Thus in three respects—development as a function of military needs, the great burdens imposed by the magnitude of the spurt, and a period of stagnation that followed it—the upsurge of the 1890s did resemble the experience of the Petrine era. At the same time, however, there were at least three important differences. Unlike the earlier case, considerable numbers of entrepreneurs, mostly native, but some foreign, were lured into activity not at all by compulsion, but by the prospect of great profits to which the State was contributing so generously. Furthermore, with the exception of communications—ports, canals and some roads—as well as mines and iron works, the Petrine period left no large stock of fixed capital; by contrast, the upsurge of the 1890s had greatly increased the fixed capital of the country. Finally, no specific obstacles for the future, comparable to serfdom of the peasantry, were produced by the spurt and left in its wake.

For these reasons, Count Witte's policies, even though they could be regarded as a failure in the short run even by sharp-sighted contemporary observers, such as for instance, Henry Adams,[18] were in reality eminently successful, because they laid the basis for the industrial performance of Russia in the second sub-period, 1906–14, during which industrial growth was resumed, though at a slightly lower rate. In that sub-period, the great withdrawal of the State from promotion of industrialization, the emergence of the banks as a source of fixed capital investment, the reduction of the burdens on the peasantry, the improvements in the position of industrial workers, at least with regard to working conditions—all these signified an abandonment of the 'Russian' features of the spurt. To return to the question, raised in my first lecture, it was possible to say now that economically speaking Russia was indeed becoming Europe. Putting the two sub-periods together, Russian experience, 1885–1914, appears as an integral part of a differentiated overall European pattern. The question then is what light does this portion of Russian industrial history cast on the history of the West? The main significance of Russian industrial experience lies in the circumstance that it completes and confirms the European pattern of industrialization. Being so much more backward than Germany, Russia offers a much more intensive and variegated pattern of substitutions, thus confirming in the first instance the basic relationship that exists at a given moment, snapshot-like, as the connection between backwardness and substitutions. But this initial corroboration is then further reinforced, dynamically as it were, when the diminished backwardness in Russia begins to create a 'German' situation there, that is to say, a situation that was peculiar to an earlier period of German industrial development. It is, therefore, in an important sense that the processes of industrial change in Russia help us better to understand the processes of change not just in Germany but in countries lying west of Russia.

At the same time, the Russian experience, and the role the State played in it, means that when we move away from our 'paradigm of three countries' and devote our attention to European countries not previously studied we are more solidly equipped for seeing the relevant problems. We are not surprised, therefore, to find that in a country like Hungary where the degree of backwardness was high, the government came to exert an influence upon industrialization, which without being as powerful as in Russia, was still considerable. And the point is not only that we know what to look for, but also are in a much better position to judge what we find to be the case.

When I approached a country such as Italy and tried to discover its position along the scale of backwardness, it was precisely with the experience of the two 'paradigm countries'—Germany and Russia—in mind. For it was quickly ascertained that Italy's degree of backwardness on the eve of its great spurt was clearly somewhere between that of Germany and Russia. Accordingly, I expected the rate of industrial growth in Italy, during its spurt of industrial growth (1896–1908), to lie somewhere between the German rate of growth in a comparable period and the Russian rate of growth in the 1890s. This expectation was indeed fulfilled, but the Italian rate proved to have been only slightly in excess of the German rate and substantially below the Russian rate. This provided the first *explicandum,* calling for a closer look at the other ingredients of the pattern. The stress on producers' goods was indeed visible, but not comparable at all to that displayed in the Russian industrialization. Nor could it be argued that comparably heavy burdens have been imposed by the industrialization upon the masses of Italian consumers. It was indeed a confirmation of expectations that the arrival of German investment banks in Italy stood at the very threshold of the spurt, and much of what happened during the years of the spurt has to be attributed to the activities of those banks. On the whole, the differences between the Italian and the Russian experience appeared larger and those between the Italian and German experience appeared smaller than would be indicated by the respective degrees of backwardness. And hence, taking my leaf from the Russian book, I had to turn to the economic policies of the Italian government during the period in question. And here I discovered that the State not only failed to follow the Russian example but on the contrary pursued a policy, particularly in the field of protectionist tariffs, which clearly slowed down the speed of growth by discriminating against those industries which had the best prospects for growth. It is, of course, not argued what policies the Italian government should have pursued. There are no doubt sufficient reasons to explain the course actually taken by reference to the strength of certain vested interests, to say nothing of the impossibility of following 'Russian' policies within a very different social and political environment. The only point that is to be made here is that the study of Italian industrialization would be less satisfactory, were it approached without

125

the benefit of knowledge of Russian experience. And this is true both for determining the original set of expectations and for appraising the results of the Italian spurt.

But the importance of the Russian paradigm is still greater when even more backward countries, such as Bulgaria and Rumania in the Balkans, are studied. For a number of reasons, the Bulgarian case appears with a good deal more clarity. Without going into details, one can state the main conclusion as follows: a rate of industrial growth quite fair by the standards of more developed countries, was obviously far below what one should expect in view of the country's degree of backwardness. It was growth unaccompanied by any significant changes in the structure of the growing industry, be it in the composition of output, or in the size of plant and enterprise, or in the productivity of labor. As in Italy, foreign banks did indeed penetrate into the country, but, unlike Italy, the German banks, despite their enormous experience in industrial investment, shied away from any involvement in industrial ventures. It is the Russian example that provides a rather convincing explanation. In Bulgarian conditions of backwardness, it appears most plausible to argue that a great spurt of industrial development fully consonant with the country's degree of backwardness could not have developed without the government's taking an active and fairly sustained initiative in promoting that development. But, except for a limited and very inadequate subsidy scheme, the Bulgarian government of the time preferred to allocate most of its budgetary means to its military expenditures, in order to satisfy its territorial aspirations towards the shores of the Aegean and in Macedonia, getting finally involved in the disastrous adventure of the second Balkan War. A different policy of the government, quite apart from its direct effects, would have provided a climate which in all likelihood would have induced the banks, either at once or after a short lapse of time, to change

126

their policy and to assimilate their activities to those they were pursuing with so much success in Italy.

This raises a methodological question which should not be allowed to pass unmentioned. A considered appraisal of the Bulgarian development and an explanation of the failure thereof in the light of the Russian experience must clearly be made against the supposition of what that development might have been, given different choices on the part of the Bulgarian State. This is what has come to be known as counter-factual history or history in the conditional mood. There is a large body of traditional historical opinion, to which also Professor Carr subscribes, which regards counter-factual history as incompatible with the true canons of historical research. This, I believe, is an untenable position, and Professor Carr's observations on the subject[19]—the alleged tendency to apply counter-factual history to recent events only or the intimation that it merely reflects the resentment of the defeated—are quite irrelevant to the understanding of the problem.

The young economic historians in the United States who have been shaping the New Economic History saw clearly that analytical apparatus of economic choice forced them into the consideration of what might have been the case. The very concept of opportunity cost inevitably propelled them in that direction. In fact, attempts have been made to push a defense of the method beyond permissible limits by arguing that any causal statement is in reality counter-factual. This is rather nonsensical, and stems from a confusion of facts, non-facts, and counter-facts. But the attempts to measure the differential contribution of an innovation or the differential effect of one set of policies actually pursued as against another set that might have been pursued in the absence of the former are altogether unexceptionable in principle and the only question is a purely practical one, that is, the degree of plausibility in operations of

127

this kind. And this will obviously vary from case to case, depending on the nature of the problem at hand.

In general, economic problems are more likely to be susceptible to such treatment, and the intrusion of non-economic factors probably tends to increase the uncertainties involved, as does consideration of more than relatively short periods. But those who oppose the counter-factual approach in history should consider that very often statements that on their face look very factual, and are light-heartedly accepted by the sworn enemies of the might-have-beens in history, are in reality as counter-factual as counter-factual can be; as is, for instance, the innocuous-looking statement that Soviet industrial output in a given year equaled, say, sixty percent of American industrial output. So is any discussion of 'errors' committed by historical figures. How can an historian criticize, say, Bruening's deflation policy during the Great Depression of the 1930s, unless he is willing to argue that a policy of credit expansion and public works would have had more positive results? In fact, even historical determinists apply the same method. When Frederic Engels explained why the absence of a certain great man would not have led to any significantly different course of events, he raised a counter-factual question in proper form, and it was only his substantive conclusions that denied the likelihood of alternatives but not the correctness of the method.

All interpretations based on comparative history are in their very essence counter-factual, as was my interpretation of Bulgarian economic history. And Professor Carr, who believes so much more strongly than I do in the enlightening force of lessons from history, should be the last man to object to the exploration of what might have been. For the so-called 'lesson' usually involves the estimation of what *would* happen in a given country, if it followed or avoided the course previously pursued in another country. There is no difference in principle be-

128

tween conditional statements of this kind for the past and those for the future. And it is some specific 'lessons for the past' that the Russian experience appears to yield for both the European industrialization as a whole and for some individual countries of the continent.

Let me repeat, however, that the enlightening force of the approach, which I have sketched out in this lecture and against which Professor Carr has directed his ill-conceived criticism, is confined to Europe as it was before the fateful year 1914. And this not only because of the difficulty of placing the Soviet industrial experience within the purview of that approach. Also West-European industrial history after 1914, and particularly after 1945, defies attempts to analyze it in terms that were appropriate to an earlier period, even though technological slack and some newly accumulated relative backwardness could be seen as the basis of the several 'economic miracles' which characterized the European scene since the end of World War II.

It is probably correct to surmise that in some measure the very recent economic history of Europe may have been influenced by the Soviet experience. In saying this I have, of course, in mind the concept of planning. But I am afraid I cannot elaborate this supposition, although to do so would be quite consonant with the basic theme of these lectures. Since I have not done any serious independent research on European economic history since 1945, I am unable to say much on the subject beyond recording my impression that Western planning has strong roots other than Russian, and that it is the general idea of expanded centralized guidance of the economy along pre-established lines rather than the actual methods, and even less the purposes of planning, that can be said to have been possibly borrowed from the Soviet Union. At any rate, also in the west of Europe new approaches, involving new hypotheses, are called for in interpreting the recent industrial history of the continent.

Those new approaches, too, will have their specific limitations. For in trying to set up interpretative models historians do not deal in universal propositions which can never be verified and can only be refuted. We deal in particular or existential propositions. It is the very nature of an historical hypothesis to constitute a set of expectations which yields enlightenment and increases the stock of our empirical knowledge within a spatially and temporally limited zone. To determine the delimitations of that zone does not mean at all a refutation of a hypothesis, but on the contrary its reinforcement as a tool of historical understanding. For this reason alone, it has been important to establish the fact that my model of European industrialization is found wanting in important respects when applied to Soviet experience. This is perhaps regrettable, and someone may be able to succeed where Professor Carr has failed and to construct an operational and more specific model of European industrial history which will meaningfully include the history of Soviet industrialization. But this, I am presumptuous enough to believe, will not necessarily detract from my approach to European industrialization and from the illumination which with the help of this approach can be derived from Russian industrial history for the history of Europe.

NOTES

LECTURE 1

1 **p. 2.** The point was often made that also most of the Slavophiles had gone through a period of 'Westernism' [*Zapadni-
chestvo*]: cf. *e.g.* Rev. George Florovskii who speaks of the
'pathos of return' of the Slavophiles from the West, in *Puti
russkogo bogosloviya* [The Ways of Russian theology] (Paris,
1937), p. 237.

2 **p. 4.** Cf. Alexander Gerschenkron, *Economic Backwardness in
Historical Perspective* (Harvard University Press, 1962),
Chap. VII, pp. 152-97.

3 **p. 5.** A. Man'kov, *Tseny i ikh dvizhenie v russkom gosudarstve
XVI veka* [Prices and their Movement in the Russian State
of the 16th Century] (Moscow, 1951).

4 **p. 5.** N. P. Pavlov-Sil'vanskii, *Feodalism v drevney Rusi*
[Feudalism in Ancient Russia] (St Petersburg, 1907), pp. 57,
80, 107; and *Feodalism v udel'noy Rusi* [Feudalism in Russia
of the Appanage Period] (St Petersburg, 1910), pp. 314, 355,
378 ff.

5 **p. 6.** Max Weber, *Wirtschaft und Gesellschaft, Grundriss der
Sozialoekonomik* (Tübingen, 1948), Vol. III, Pt 1, p. 148.

6 **p. 6.** For criticism of Pavlov-Sil'vanskii, including that of
the specific points mentioned in the text, cf. N. Kareev, *V
kakom smysle mozhno govorit' o sushestvovanii feodalisma v
Rossii? Po povodu teorii Pavlova-Sil'vanskogo* [In What Sense
is it Possible to Speak of the Existence of Feudalism in
Russia? About the Theory of Pavlov-Sil'vanskii] (St Petersburg, 1910), pp. 107-8; and P. B. Struve, 'Sushestvoval li v
drevney Rusi feodal'nyi pravoporyadok?' ['Did Feudal Legal
Order Exist in Ancient Russia?'] in *Sostsial'naya i economi-
cheskaya istoriya Rossii* [Social and Economic History of
Russia] (Paris, 1952), pp. 222, 233 ff.

7 **p. 6.** Marc Bloch, *Feudal Society*, translated from the French
by L. A. Manyon, foreword by M. M. Postan (London, 1961),
p. 56.

8 **p. 6.** M. Tugan-Baranovskii, *Russkaya fabrika v proshlom i
nastoyashchem, Istoriko-ekonomicheskoye izsledovanie.* Vol. I:

Istoricheskoe razvitie russkoy fabriki v XIX veke [Russian Factory in its Past and Present, an Historico-Economic Study. Vol. I: The Historical Development of the Russian Factory in the 19th Century] (St Petersburg, 1898).

9 **p. 7.** E. Tarle, 'Byla li Ekaterininskaya Rossiya ekonomi-cheski-otstaloy stranoy?' ['Was Russia of Catherine the Great Economically Backward?'] in *Sovremennyi Mir* [The Contemporary World], No. 5 (1910), pp. 3-29. Reprinted in E. V. Tarle, *Zapad i Rossiya* [The West and Russia] (St Petersburg, 1918), pp. 122-49.

10 **p. 8.** Marc Bloch, *op. cit.* p. 56.

11 **p. 9.** Max Weber, *The Protestant Ethic and the Spirit of Capitalism* (New York–London, 1950).

12 **p. 9.** *Ibid.* p. 222.

13 **p. 10.** Werner Sombart, *Der moderne Kapitalismus*, Vol. I: 2 (Munich–Leipzig, 1928), p. 881.

14 **p. 10.** Kurt Samuelsson, *Ekonomi och religion* (Stockholm, 1957).

15 **p. 10.** Max Weber, *The Protestant Ethic*, p. 72.

16 **p. 13.** Cf. *Le Stoglav ou les cent chapitres*, ed. E. Duchesne (Paris, 1920), pp. xxxiii-xxxv, 83, 87-9, 104, 132-3.

17 **p. 13.** Cf. Father Florovskii, *op. cit.* pp. 23-4.

18 **p. 14.** Cf. Father Florovskii, *op. cit.* p. 63: 'The reform was decided and thought through in the Palace.'

19 **p. 14.** Cf. V. O. Kliuchevskii, *Sochineniya* [Works] (Moscow, 1957), Vol. III, p. 307.

20 **p. 14.** Since in the years to come the Old Believers refused to regard the *Stoglav* 'as though it never were' and eagerly referred to its decisions in upholding their tenets, there emerged for some time a tendency among the theological defenders of the established Church to deny the official character of the *Stoglav* canons and even their authenticity: cf. V. Bocharev's, *Stoglav i istoriya sobora 1551 goda* [*Stoglav* and the History of the 1551 Council] (Yukhnov, 1906), who deals with the problem in Chapter XVIII. In fact, as early as 1876, Kliuchevskii in a sharp review of a German study emphasized that 'on the basis of irrefutable historical evidence' it was proven that the canons of the *Stoglav* had been 'unconditionally recognized by the secular government and were made public in the accepted forms as the decisions of the council, that is to say, as the ecclesiastic law of the land'. (Cf. V. O. Kliuchevskii, *Otsyvy i rechi* [Reviews and Speeches] (St Petersburg, 1918), pp. xxiii-xxiv.

21 **p. 15.** Cf. A. I. Klibanov, *Reformatsionnye dvizheniya v Rossii*

v XIV–pervoy polovine XVI vekakh [Reformation Movements in Russia in the 14th Century to the First Half of the 16th Century] (Moscow, 1960). The purpose of his study, Klibanov says, is to refute the alleged historical contrast between Russia and the West, created in the era of Reformation and Humanism when the West had discovered 'the free man' and 'the sovereign individual', whereas Russia has remained for ever alien to the ideas of liberty and respect for man. 'The complete picture of Russian intellectual history will reveal Russia's real place in the general development of European culture and will cause many disappointments to the bourgeois propounders of Russian cultural separatedness' (pp. 4 and 296).

22   **p. 16.** Cf. A. I. Klibanov, *op. cit.* p. 4.

23   **p. 16.** N. Vasilenko, 'Raskol' ['The Schism'] in *Entsiklopedicheskii Slovar'* [Encyclopædic Dictionary] (Brokgauz-Efron, St Petersburg, 1899), Vol. 51, p. 290.

24   **p. 17.** Cf. Nikolai Kostomarov, 'Istoriya raskola u raskol'nikov' ['The Schismatics' History of the Schism'] in *Istoricheskie monografii i izsledovaniya* [Historical Monographs and Studies] (St Petersburg, 1872), Vol. 12, p. 419.

25   **p. 17.** V. O. Kliuchevskii, *op. cit.* Vol. III, p. 285.

26   **p. 17.** Rev. Sergii Bulgakov, *Pravoslavie, Ocherki ucheniya pravoslavnoy tserkvi* [The Orthodoxy, Outlines of the Doctrine of the Orthodox Church] (Paris, n.d.), p. 373.

27   **p. 18.** P. I. Lyashchenko, *Istoriya narodnogo khozyaystva S.S.S.R.* [History of the National Economy of the U.S.S.R.] (Moscow, 1948), Vol. II.

28   **p. 19.** See B. B. Kafengauz and N. I. Pavlenko, *Ocherki istorii S.S.S.R.; Period feodalisma; Rossiya v pervoy chetverti XVIII veka; Preobrazovaniya Petra I* [Essays in the History of the U.S.S.R.; Period of Feudalism; Russia in the First Quarter of the 18th Century; Reforms of Peter I] (Moscow, 1954), p. 381; and P. N. Miliukov, *Ocherki po istorii russkoy kultury* [Essays in the History of Russian Culture], Vol. II (Paris, 1931), p. 81.

29   **p. 21.** On the economic activities of the Old Believers, cf. Gerhart von Schulze-Gaevernitz, *Volkswirtschaftliche Studien aus Russland* (Leipzig, 1899), particularly pp. 76-7 and 86 ff.; P. A. Buryshkin, *Moskva kupecheskaya* [The Merchants' Moscow] (New York, 1954), *passim*; *Istoriya Moskvy* [The History of Moscow] (Moscow, 1954), Vol. III, pp. 177-294 and p. 318; Anatole Leroy-Beaulieu, *The Empire of the Tsars and the Russians* (New York–London, 1902), pp. 336-42; P. A. Berlin, *Russkaya burzhuaziya v staroe i novoe vremya* [The Russian

Bourgeoisie in Old and Modern Times] (Moscow, 1922), pp. 92, 108-9, 185-6; P. Usov, 'Pavel Ivanovich Mel'nikov, Ego zhizn' i literaturnaya deyatel'nost' ['P. I. Mel'nikov, His Life and Literary Work'], in *Polnoe Sobranie Sochinenii P. I. Mel'nikova* [Complete Collected Works of P. I. Mel'nikov] (in the following, referred to as 'Mel'nikov, *Works*') (14 vols. St Petersburg–Moscow, 1897–8), Vol. i, *passim*; P. I. Mel'-nikov, 'Ocherki Popovshchiny' ['Essays on the Priest Branch of Old Believers'], *Works*, Pt i, Vol. 13 (St Petersburg and Moscow, 1898), and Pt ii, Vol. 14 (St Petersburg and Moscow, 1898); P. I. Mel'nikov, *Na gorakh* [On the Hills], *Works*, Vols. 7, 8, 9, and 10 (St Petersburg–Moscow, 1898); P. I. Mel'nikov, *V lesakh* [In the Forests], *Works*, Vols. 3, 4, 5, and 6 (St Petersburg–Moscow, 1897); Tugan-Baranovskii, *Russkaya Fabrika . . . op. cit.* pp. 98, 296.

LECTURE 2

1 **p. 23.** Cf. V. G. Druzhinin, *Raskol na Donu v kontse XVII veka* [The Schism in the Don Region at the End of the 17th Century] (St Petersburg, 1889).

2 **p. 24.** Cf. Ivan Stchoukine, *Le Suicide collectif dans le raskol russe* (Paris, 1903).

3 **p. 24.** V. O. Kliuchevskii, *Sochineniya* [Works], Vol. iii, *Kurs russkoy istorii* [A Course on Russian History], Pt iii (Moscow, 1957), p. 355.

4 **p. 25.** M. Gorchakov, 'Sinod' ['Synod'], *Entsiklopedicheskii Slovar'* [Encyclopædic Dictionary] (Brokgauz-Efron, St Petersburg, 1900), Vol. 59, pp. 38-43; P. V. Verkhovskoy, *Uchrezhdenie dukhovnoy kollegii i dukhovnyi reglament* [The Establishment of the Ecclesiastic Collegium and the Ecclesiastic Ordinance] (Rostov on Don, 1916), Vols. i and ii; also, P. N. Miliukov, *Ocherki po istorii russkoy kultury* [Essays in the History of Russian Culture], Vol. ii (Paris, 1931), p. 179.

5 **p. 25.** Cf. the complaints of Metropolitan Anthony in P. V. Verkhovskoy, *op. cit.* Vol. i, p. cli.

6 **p. 25.** P. V. Verkhovskoy, *op. cit.* Vol. i, p. 658.

7 **p. 26.** Antonii Possevini, S.J., *Moscovia* (Antwerp, 1587), p. 193: 'Cum Angli mercatores eidem obtulissent librum quo hereticus quidam ostendere conabatur Pontificem Maximum esse Antichristum.'

8 **p. 27.** Father Florovskii, *op. cit.* p. 67. Similarly, Ivan Stchoukine (*op. cit.* p. 98) who says: 'Ainsi toute la doctrine

des raskolniks se concentra dans l'idée des persécutions de
l'antéchrist'; and also Nikolai Berdyaev in *Russkaya ideya*
[The Russian Idea] (Paris, 1946), pp. 45-6. It is difficult to
accept these views which generalize and magnify out of all
proportion an element of Old Belief whose historical significance was in the main limited both in time and in space; and
to the extent that it was not so limited those views convert the
extreme views of little groups—what Berdyaev himself calls
'the left wing of the Schism' or 'its farthest periphery' (*ibid.*)
—into the general ideology of the Old Believers. It is an
understandable desire on the part of those interested in the
intellectual and spiritual history of Russia to build the Old
Belief into that history. But this cannot be achieved except
at the price of exaggerations and distortions. The belief in the
mythical city of Kitezh, populated by the righteous, hidden
under the waters of a lake and representing the kingdom of
true and pure faith, does not explain the behavior of Old
Believers in the non-mythical towns and villages of the
Russian tsardom.

9 p. 27. Cf. *Entsiklopedicheskii Slovar'* (Brokgauz-Efron, St
Petersburg, 1896), Vol. 38, p. 84.

10 p. 27. Baron von Haxthausen, *The Russian Empire, Its
People, Institutions and Resources* (London, 1856), Vol. I, p. 529.

11 p. 27. On the Astrakhan uprising, cf. *Khrestomatiya po istorii
S.S.S.R.* [Readings in the History of the U.S.S.R.], ed. S. S.
Dmitriev and M. V. Nechkina, Vol. II (Moscow, 1949), p. 48.
On the Don uprising, cf. V. I. Lebedev, *Bulavinskoe vosstanie*
[Bulavin's Uprising] (Moscow, 1967), p. 63 and for the text
of the *Prelestnye pis'ma*—the inflammatory appeals to the
people by Bulavin and by his successor Golyi, cf. pp. 87-
95. On the role of Old Believers among the leaders of the
rebellion, cf. *Bulavinskoe vosstanie*, Trudy istoriko-arkheo-
graficheskogo instituta Akademii Nauk S.S.S.R. [Works of
the Historical-Paleogeographical Institute of the Academy
of Sciences of the U.S.S.R.] (Moscow, 1935), Vol. XII, p. 58.

12 p. 27. Cf. B. B. Kafengauz and N. I. Pavlenko, *Ocherki istorii
S.S.S.R.; Period feodalisma; Rossiya v pervoy chetverti XVIII
veka; Preobrazovaniya Petra I* [Essays in the History of the
U.S.S.R.; Period of Feudalism; Russia in the First Quarter
of the 18th Century; Reforms of Peter I] (Moscow, 1954),
p. 254; also V. I. Lebedev, *op. cit.* p. 68.

13 p. 29. Cf. *Pugachevshchina* [The Pugachev Uprising], Vol. I,
Iz arkhiva Pugacheva [From Pugachev's Archive] (Moscow–
Leningrad, 1926), pp. 32-3, and 40; V. U. Mavrodin, *Krest'yan-*

skaya voyna v Rossii v 1773–1775 godakh, Vosstanie Pugacheva
[The Peasant War in Russia, 1773–1775, Pugachev's Uprising]
(Leningrad, 1966), Vol. ii, pp. 67-89.

14 **p. 30.** P. V. Verkhovskoy, *op. cit.* Vol. i, p. cl, and pp. 625-6.
By the edicts the official use of the offensive term Schism was
terminated; praying houses that had been closed down were
unsealed; confiscated properties were returned; new praying
houses and even churches with bells could be built; the Old
Believers' clergy was freed from taxation and conscription,
and marriage ceremonies conducted by them were officially
recognized. The tolerance edicts quite naturally led to a
movement within the established Church to lessen its bureaucratic regimen and to re-introduce the institution of Church
Councils.

15 **p. 30.** Obviously an estimate of the numerical strength of a
persecuted group cannot be much more than guesswork.
Because of ignorance and deliberate distortion, the official
figures cannot be taken seriously at all. They showed a near
constancy in the numbers of Old Believers between 1826 and
1864. As was convincingly demonstrated by Mel'nikov, the
probable actual figure must have been about ten times higher,
amounting to about 10,000,000 in the mid-sixties of the last
century. Cf. Mel'nikov, 'Schislenie Raskol'nikov' ['Counting
the Schismatics'], *Works*, Vol. 14 (St Petersburg–Moscow,
1898), pp. 332-95. Even 10,000,000 was likely to have been an
underestimate. It is probable that in the first decades of the
twentieth century the Old Believers constituted at least one-
third of the total Great Russian population (to which latter
group alone their numbers should be related). A recent Soviet
author gives a figure of 20-25,000,000 Old Believers for the
time preceding the October Revolution. Cf. F. Fedorenko,
Sekty, ich vera i dela [The Sects, Their Faith and Deeds]
(Moscow, 1965), p. 102. By extrapolating from the 1897 census
one obtains a number of Great Russian population at the
time of about 60,000,000. The number of Old Believers under
Peter the Great was estimated at about 500,000 out of a
Great Russian population of 10,000,000. Cf. Usov, 'Pavel
Ivanovich Mel'nikov . . .' in Mel'nikov, *Works*, Vol. i (St
Petersburg–Moscow, 1897), p. 174. I have computed the
numbers of Great Russians at Peter's time from V. M. Kabu-
san, *Narodoselenie Rossii v XVIII–pervoy polovine XIX veka*
[Russia's Population in the 18th Century and the First Half
of the 19th Century] (Moscow, 1963), pp. 159-61. This would
mean that while the Great Russian population increased *six*

fold between the Petrine Period and the twentieth century, the number of Old Believers was about *forty times* larger in our century than in the first quarter of the eighteenth century.

16   **p. 30.** Father Florovskii, *op. cit.* p. 162. The statement by Shishkov is all the more revealing as he considered Church-Slavonic and Russian to be identical languages.

17   **p. 31.** P. I. Mel'nikov, 'Schislenie raskol'nikov', *op. cit.* p. 390.

18   **p. 33.** Georg Simmel, *Soziologie, Untersuchung ueber die Formen der Vergesellschaftung* (Berlin, 1958), pp. 494-5.

19   **p. 34.** N. I. Kapterev, *Patriarch Nikon i tsar' Alexei Mikhailovich* [Patriarch Nikon and Tsar Alexis] (Sergiev Posad, 1909), Vol. I, pp. 381-2.

20   **p. 34.** This was the previously mentioned Kokorev; cf. V. A. Kokorev, 'Economicheskie provaly, po vospominaniyam s 1837 goda' [Economic Disasters, according to Reminiscences from 1837 on'], in *Russkii Arkhiv*, No. 2 (St Petersburg, 1887), pp. 252-3.

21   **p. 35.** Cf. Nicolai Kostomarov, 'Istoriya raskola u raskol'-nikov' ['The Schismatics' History of the Schism'], *Istoricheskie monografii i izsledovaniya* [Historical Monographs and Studies] (St Petersburg, 1872), Vol. 12, pp. 423-4 and p. 431.

22   **p. 37.** In the light of the great popularity of the book of Jesus, the son of Sirach (Ecclesiasticus) with the Old Believers, it is significant that Max Weber stresses the 'traditional' spirit of the book and mentions the attachment to it of conservative Lutheran peasants in Germany—cf. Max Weber, *Protestant Ethic*, p. 164.

23   **p. 37.** P. N. Miliukov, *Ocherki po istorii russkoy kultury* [Essays in the History of Russian Culture], Vol. III (St Petersburg, 1909), p. 174.

24   **p. 37.** Everett E. Hagen, *On the Theory of Social Change, How Economic Growth Begins* (London, 1964). For references to Old Believers, cf. pp. 188, 217, 235, and 248.

25   **p. 38.** Cf. Alexander Gerschenkron, *Continuity in History and Other Essays* (Harvard University Press, 1968), pp. 368-74.

26   **p. 39.** Cf. on the preceding: A. A. Kizevetter, 'Politicheskaya tendentsiya drevnerusskago Domostroya' [The Political Tendency of the Ancient-Russian *Domostroy*'], in *Istoricheskie ocherki* [Historical Essays] (Moscow, 1912), pp. 3-28 and particularly pp. 5, 18-25. For the text of *Domostroy*, cf. A. Orlov (ed.), *Domostroy po konshinskomu spisku i podobnym* [*Domostroy* according to Konshin's and Similar Copies] (Moscow, 1908): Russian Reprint Series, XXXVII (The Hague, 1967, Pt II, Chaps. 15 (p. 13), 17 (p. 14), and 38 (pp. 37-8).

E. Duchesne in his French translation of *Domostroy* renders the Russian *rany vozlagati* by 'inflict blows' [*coups*] but this is surely unwarranted—cf. *Le Domostroy, traduction et commentaire* (Paris, 1910), p. 154.

27　p. 39. N. I. Kostomarov, 'Ocherk domashney zhizni i nravov velikorusskago naroda v XVI i XVII stoletiyakh i starinnye zemskie sobory' ['An Outline of Home Life and Mores of Great Russian People in the XVI and XVII Centuries and the Ancient Councils of the Land'], *Sobranie Sochinenii* [Collected Works] (St Petersburg, 1906), p. 136. Cf. also V. O. Kliuchevskii, *Pis'ma k P. P. Gvozdevu, 1861–70* [Letters to Gvozdev] (Moscow, 1924), p. 71.

28　p. 39. The particular harshness of the Russian translation of the passage is worth noting. What the Russian text renders as 'crush his ribs' appears in the English text of the Ecclesiasticus in the Catholic Bible as 'beat his sides' and even the Jerusalem Bible (New York, 1966, p. 1,076) does not go beyond 'bruising the ribs'. Note furthermore that the *Domostroy*, too, spoke of 'crushing the ribs' (cf. A. Orlov, *op. cit.* Chap. 17, p. 15).

29　p. 39. The best descriptions of Old Believers' family life are contained in the four long volumes of the two 'ethnographic novels' by P. I. Mel'nikov—*Na gorakh* [On the Hills] and *V lesakh* [In the Forests]. Mel'nikov, to whom reference was made previously, had a profound knowledge of the group. From a civil servant engaged in repressions he developed into a rather sympathetic and sharp-eyed observer. The figures he presents in his novels are mostly taken from real life, and the novels, although not entirely destitute of artistic merits, are much more in the nature of anthropological reports than actual works of fiction.

30　p. 40. *Zhitie protopopa Avvakuma* [The Life of Archpriest Avvakum] (Moscow, 1960), pp. 59-60 and 87.

31　p. 40. A. P. Shchapov, 'Zemstvo i raskol' ['The Zemstvo and the Schism'], in *Sochineniya* [Works] (2 vols. St Petersburg, 1906), Vol. ɪ, p. 502.

32　p. 40. A. P. Shchapov, 'Russkii raskol staroobryadstva, razsmatrivaemyi v svyazi s vnutrennim sostoyaniem russkoy tserkvi i grazhdanostvennosti v XVII veke i pervoy polovine XVIII veka; opyt istoricheskago izsledovaniya o prichinakh proizkhozhdeniya i razprostraneniya russkago raskola' ['The Russian Schism of the Old Belief, Considered in Connection with the Internal State of the Russian Church and Civil Order in the 17th Century and the First Half of the 18th Century;

an Essay of an Historical Exploration of the Causes of the Origin and Diffusion of the Russian Schism'], in *Sochineniya* [Works] (St Petersburg, 1906). For Shchapov the Schism contains, under the cover of a mystical and apocalyptic symbolism, the negation of the reform of Peter the Great, a rebellion against the foreign elements in Russian life, resistance against the empire and the government, bold protest against censuses of souls, taxes and multiplicity of tributes, against conscription, serfdom, local authorities . . . cf. Vol. i, p. 173.

33 p. 40. A. P. Shchapov, 'Znachenie zhenshchiny v antropologicheskom i sotsial'nom razvitii russkoy narodnosti' ['The Significance of the Woman in the Anthropological and Social Evolution of the Russian Nationality'] in *Sochineniya* [Works] (St Petersburg, 1906), Vol. ii, p. 35; and 'Polozhenie zhenshchiny v rossii po do-petrovskamu vozreniiu' ['The Condition of the Woman in Russia According to pre-Petrine Views'] *op. cit.* Vol. ii, p. 113.

34 p. 40. A. P. Shchapov, *Sochineniya* [Works], Vol. ii, p. 134. I might mention here, however, for what it is worth, that in Maxim Gorky's novel *Foma Gordeev*, it is the second wife, an Old Believer not from the north but from the Urals, who refuses to be beaten up by her husband, a barbarous drunken Volga merchant. In this she is quite unlike the man's first wife, a member of the established Church, who became sterile as the result of her husband's beatings.

35 p. 40. Cf. D. Richter in *Entsiklopedicheskii Slovar'* (Brokgauz-Efron), St Petersburg, 1907, Supplement, *Rossiya*, Vol. 4, p. vii.

36 p. 41. Cf. S. V. Maksimov, *Sobranie Sochinenii* [Collected Works] (St Petersburg, n.d.), Vol. xx, p. 142.

37 p. 41. P. A. Buryshkin, *Moskva kupecheskaya* [The Merchants' Moscow] (New York, 1954), p. 204.

38 p. 41. Cf. Alexander Gerschenkron, *Economic Backwardness in Historical Perspective* (Cambridge, Mass., 1962), p. 61, and Alexander Gerschenkron, *Continuity in History and Other Essays* (Cambridge, Mass., 1968), p. 138.

39 p. 43. Baron von Haxthausen, *op. cit.* pp. 287-8. Subsequently it was reported that a sect which venerated Napoleon as the Son of God still existed in the second half of the nineteenth century (cf. Usov, *op. cit.* p. 175).

40 p. 43. Nicolai Kostomarov, 'Istoriya raskola u raskol'nikov', *loc. cit.* p. 383.

41 p. 44. Max Weber, *Wirtschaft und Gesellschaft, op. cit.* p. 304.

42   **p. 44.** Max Weber, *The Sociology of Religion*, with an introduction by Talcott Parsons (London, 1963), p. lix.

43   **p. 45.** Cf. Father Florovskii, *op. cit.* p. 84.

44   **p. 45.** Father Florovskii, *op. cit.* pp. 82, 84 and 88. Also P. V.
Verkhovskoy, *op. cit.* p. 85.

45   **p. 46.** Sir William Petty, 'Political Arithmetic', *Economic
Writings* (Cambridge, 1899), Vol. i, p. 264.

46   **p. 46.** Max Weber, *Protestant Ethic . . .*, *op. cit.* p. 179 and
pp. 43, 189, 279, 282.

47   **p. 46.** Werner Sombart, *Der moderne Kapitalismus* (Munich–
Leipzig 1928), Vol. i: 2, Chap. 60, 'Die Ketzer', p. 881.

48   **p. 46.** Schulze-Gaevernitz, *op. cit.* pp. 76-7.

49   **p. 48.** It used to be assumed that Krizhanich had spent some
time studying in Vienna itself, but Jagić showed that there
was no evidence for that: cf. Vatroslav Jagić, *Zivot i rad
Jurja Križanića* [Life and Work of Juraj Križanić] (Zagreb,
1917), p. 16.

50   **p. 49.** For the text of Krizhanich's memorandum, cf. Sergei
A. Belokurov, *Iz dukhovnoy zhizni moskovskago obshchestva
XVII veka* [From the Spiritual Life of Moscow Society of the
17th Century] (Moscow, 1903), Vol. ii, pp. 87-106 (particularly
pp. 100-6).

51   **p. 50.** Cf. S. A. Belokurov, *op. cit.* Vol. i, pp. 152-9.

52   **p. 50.** V. O. Kliuchevskii, *op. cit.* Vol. iii, pp. 301 and 329-33.

53   **p. 50.** For the most recent English edition, cf. *The Travels of
Olearius in 17th-Century Russia*, translated and edited by
Samuel H. Baron (Stanford, 1967).

54   **p. 51.** S. A. Belokurov, *op. cit.* Vol. i, p. 182.

55   **p. 51.** S. M. Solov'ev, *Istoriya Rossii s drevneyshikh vremen*
[History of Russia from Ancient Times] (St Petersburg,
Edition Obshchestvennaya Pol'za, n.d.), Book iii, Vol. 13,
pp. 785-6; S. A. Belokurov, *op. cit.* Vol. i, p. 181.

56   **p. 51.** Cf. Vatroslav Jagić, *op. cit.* pp. 12-13.

57   **p. 51.** Cf. S. A. Belokurov, Vol. ii, p. 92. Also Olearius, whose
book Krizhanich apparently had brought along to Russia,
spoke of Russian intolerance towards catholics (*Olearius, op.
cit.* p. 277).

58   **p. 51.** Solov'ev regarded Krizhanich's catholicism as the main
reason for his banishment: 'Krizhanich could not hide that
he was of Latin faith and even a Latin priest. The learned
Serbian came at a wrong time, and the uninvited teacher was
exiled to Siberia . . .' because of his 'unorthodoxy' [*nepravo-
slavie*]: cf. S. M. Solov'ev, *Istoriya Rossii . . ., op. cit.* pp. 785-6.
Solov'ev was mistaken in calling Krizhanich a Serbian. The

correct facts of Krizhanich's biography became known rather slowly.

59 **p. 52.** S. A. Belokurov, *op. cit.* Vol. I, p. 236.

60 **p. 52.** Cf. *e.g.* S. M. Solov'ev (*Istoriya Rossii, op. cit.* Vol. 13, p. 778), who called Krizhanich 'an ardent Slavic patriot'; and similarly Kliuchevskii's characterization of Krizhanich: 'A little bit of a philosopher and theologian, a little bit of an economist, a great philologist, but above all a patriot, to be more precise, an ardent Pan-Slavist, because for him the true fatherland was not any historically known state, but the united Slavdom.' Cf. V. O. Kliuchevskii, *Sochineniya* [Works] (Moscow, 1957), p. 245; or Jensen's chapter on 'Den förste store panslavisten' in Alfred Jensen, *Rysk Kulturhistoria* (Stockholm, 1908), Vol. I, pp. 157-70. For a Soviet view, cf. B. D. Datsiuk, *Yurii Krizhanich* (Moscow, 1946).

61 **p. 53.** Miliukov even suggests that Krizhanich could have remained in Moscow and avoided the exile at the price of forswearing his catholicism. But there seems to be no evidence in support of this statement. Cf. P. N. Miliukov, *Ocherki po istorii russkoy kultury* [Essays in the History of Russian Culture] (St Petersburg, 1909), Vol. III, p. 115. It has been said that Krizhanich would not have objected to becoming Greek Orthodox if it had not been for the requirement of being re-baptized in the process. But this requirement was rescinded by the Council of 1666, that is to say, five years after Krizhanich's deportation and a full decade before the end of his exile. Cf. V. Valdenberg, *Gosudarstvennye idei Krizhanicha* [Krizhanich's Ideas on the State] (St Petersburg, 1912), p. 33.

62 **p. 53.** Yurii Krizhanich, *Politika* (*Razgovory ob wladatelystwu*) (Moscow, 1965). This edition contains both the original text in Krizhanich's hybrid Slavic and the Russian translation.

63 **p. 53.** Yurii Krizhanich, *Politika, op. cit.* p. 704.

64 **p. 53.** Cf. Vatroslav Jagić's chapter on Krizhanich's erudition [*nacitanost*], *op. cit.* pp. 482 ff.

65 **p. 54.** This criticism of Russian absolutism has been particularly stressed in the literature: cf. Valdenberg, *op. cit.* p. 241; P. N. Miliukov, *Ocherki . . ., op. cit.* Vol. III, p. 126; G. V. Plekhanov, 'Istoriya russkoy obshchestvennoy mysli' ['History of Russian Social Ideas'], in *Sochineniya* [Works], Vol. XX (Book I, Pt II), p. 289.

66 **p. 55.** Cf. *The Travels of Olearius, op. cit.* pp. 126-54.

67 **p. 56.** For Krizhanich on Herberstein, cf. *Politika, op. cit.* p. 448. For Herberstein's strictures, *e.g.* of commercial dishonesty

141

of the Russians, cf. Sigismund zu Herberstein, *Reise zu den Moskowitern 1526* (Munich, 1966), p. 160.

68   **p. 57.** 'Die protestantischen Sekten und der Geist des Kapitalismus', in Max Weber, *Gesammelte Aufsaetze zur Religionssoziologie* (Tübingen, 1947), Vol. i, pp. 235-6.

69   **p. 58.** John Galsworthy, *The Man of Property*, Chap. 5, in *The Forsyte Saga* (New York, 1934), p. 140; Raymond Queneau, *Zazie dans le métro* (Paris, 1959), p. 232.

70   **p. 58.** Max Weber, 'Die protestantischen Sekten', *op. cit.* p. 219.

71   **p. 60.** As previously mentioned, Soviet historiography has been anxious to show that Russian history contained all the elements of its Western counterpart. To some extent, this tendency has been the result of the basic attitude of Marxian scholarship as formed in the years of the Great Debate of the 1890s; at the same time, it undoubtedly also stemmed from the nationalistic desire to show that historically Russia has been just as well provided as the European West. *V Gretsii vse est'*—Greece has everything—says an old semi-russified Greek in one of Chekhov's well-known stories. It appears that particularly in Stalin's time Russian scholars were under compulsion to sustain this claim of the country's all-comprehensive historical endowment. It would be difficult otherwise to understand why the great historian of ancient Russian handicraft, B. A. Rybakov, was willing to mar his splendid book by inserting in its concluding sections a disquisition on Russian craft guilds, voluntarily formed, in the fourteenth and fifteenth centuries. Actually, all the evidence Rybakov possesses refers to a single craft of the blacksmiths, who are said to have had craft churches and common feasts. He goes on to admit the lack of 'direct indications' for the existence of formal organizational structures, and then says: 'The sources of the following epoch [sixteenth-seventeenth centuries] contain a number of disjointed data concerning elements on the craft-guild system in Russian cities. Very often these elements are in a state of decay which may be considered as evidence for their somewhat prolonged evolution in the preceding period.' This inference *ex nihilo* is, of course, fairly amazing, and so is the final conclusion for the sake of which, it would seem, the foregoing irrelevancies have been presented: 'The Russian handicraft was subject to general historical laws that were compulsory [sic] both for the West and the East. But at the same time it proceeded along an independent path, creating values bearing the clear stamp of creativity of the Russian people.' Cf. B. A. Rybakov, *Remeslo drevney Rusi* [Handicraft in Ancient Russia] (Moscow, 1948), pp. 766, 775, and 782. The Soviet dictatorship has exacted much heavier tributes from scholars and scholarship than the mere addition of a few ludicrous pages to a great work. Still, Rybakov deserves our sympathy. At any rate, he has not provided a shred of evidence to disprove the statements in the text concerning the lack of craft-guild experience from Russian economic history.

LECTURE 3

1   **p. 62.** Joseph A. Schumpeter, *History of Economic Analysis* (New York, 1954), pp. 147 and 335.

2   **p. 62.** Eli F. Heckscher, *Mercantilism* (London, 1935), p. 19.

3   **p. 62.** Goethe, *Maximen und Reflexionen, Schriften zur Naturwissenschaft*, Pt I, *Saemtliche Werke, Jubilaeumsausgabe*, Vol. XXXIX, p. 72.

4   **p. 63.** Jacob Viner, *Studies in the Theory of International Trade* (New York, 1937), Chaps. I and II, and p. 109 for the phrase quoted.

5   **p. 64.** J. A. Schumpeter, *op. cit.* pp. 344-5, 350, 361, and 376.

6   **p. 64.** John Maynard Keynes, *The General Theory of Employment, Interest and Money* (London, 1936), p. 335.

7   **p. 65.** Eli F. Heckscher, *op. cit.* p. 20.

8   **p. 65.** 'Nation-state' is a concept that should be used with much greater hesitation than is usually done in literature. In American and French usage state and nation are nearly synonymous; in German and Russian usage they are not, but in that usage the empirical counterpart of the concept 'nation-state' is quite blurred. In Europe, the Scandinavian countries and Portugal do indeed appear to be nation-states. Austria-Hungary, Switzerland, Belgium, and Russia for that matter do not fit the concept at all, and Britain's relation to it is quite uncertain. Thus the concept is either pleonastic or, in a large number of cases, empirically wrong. For both lexical and historical reasons it would seem advisable to abstain from the use of so questionable a term.

9   **p. 65.** William Cunningham, *The Growth of English Industry and Commerce in Modern Times* (Cambridge, 1892), pp. 17, 103.

10 **p. 66.** Harald Hjärne, 'Nya problem för världshistorisk framställning', *Samlade skrifter* (Stockholm, 1940), Vol. IV, p. 275.

11   p. 67. 'Karl XII från europeisk synpunkt', *Samlade skrifter* (Stockholm, 1932), Vol. II, p. 279.

12   p. 67. Cf. *e.g.*, Franz von Liszt, *Das Voelkerrecht, systematisch dargestellt* (Berlin, 1902), p. 4; Alfred Verdross, *Voelkerrecht* (Vienna, 1950), pp. 33-5. It is another matter that the concept of Christian-European States of the West as members of the community of nations was extended, long before Hjärne wrote, first to the whole of Christian Europe; that then the inclusion of the United States destroyed the exclusive European character of the community; and that since Turkey's admission to the concert of powers in 1856 also the adjective 'Christian' was no longer applicable. The original concept still lingered on in treatises on international law well into the twentieth century.

13   p. 67. Eli F. Heckscher, *op. cit.* p. 13.

14   p. 67. Eli F. Heckscher, *op. cit.* p. 23.

15   p. 67. Eli F. Heckscher, 'Mercantilism', *Economic History Review*, No. 7 (1936), p. 44.

16   p. 69. Alexander Gerschenkron, 'On the Concept of Continuity in History', *Continuity in History and Other Essays* (Harvard University Press, 1968), pp. 11-39.

17   p. 71. Cf. Martin Wolfe, 'French Views on Wealth and Taxes from the Middle Ages to the Old Regime', *The Journal of Economic History, The Tasks of Economic History*, Vol. XXVI, No. 4 (December, 1966), pp. 473-4.

18   p. 72. E. I. Zaozerskaya, *Manufaktura pri Petre I* [Manufactures under Peter I] (Moscow–Leningrad, 1947), p. 9. See also Note 20 below.

19   p. 72. In his thoughtful lecture on mercantilism, Professor Wilson says: 'It would be rash, nevertheless, to dismiss too hastily the possibility that the economic growth of the period owed something to the remarkable concentration of human energy and organized effort we call the mercantile system' (Charles Wilson, *Mercantilism* (London, 1958), p. 27). This cautious language, to my mind, is much too restrained with regard to mercantilism in general, but it is totally inapplicable to the experience of Russian mercantilism.

20   p. 73. E. I. Zaozerskaya, 'Manufaktura', in *Ocherki istorii S.S.S.R., Period feodalisma* [Essays in the History of the U.S.S.R., Period of Feudalism] (Moscow, 1954), p. 102. In this essay the number of Petrine mills was further reduced by the author (as compared with her own previous estimate) from 200 to 178. Cf. E. I. Zaozerskaya, *Manufaktura pri Petre I* [Manufacture under Peter I] (Moscow–Leningrad,

1947), pp. 9-10. In fact, it appears that some further considerable reductions of the number may be in order.

21   p. 74. P. N. Miliukov, *Gosudarstvennoe khozyaystvo Rossii v
pervoy chetverti XVIII stoletiya i reforma Petra Velikago*
[Russia's State Economy in the First Quarter of the 18th
Century and the Reform of Peter the Great] (St Petersburg,
1905), p. 485.

22   p. 74. S. G. Strumilin, *Ocherki ekonomicheskoy istorii Rossii*
[Essays in Russian Economic History] (Moscow, 1960), pp.
318-30.

23   p. 74. P. N. Miliukov, *Gosudarstvennoe khozyaystvo, op. cit.
passim.*

24   p. 75. V. O. Kliuchevskii, *op. cit.* Vol. III, p. 236.

25   p. 75. What follows is based as far as possible on the previously
cited work of S. G. Strumilin (*Ocherki ekonomicheskoy istorii
Rossii*) and the page numbers in parentheses refer to that
volume. Strumilin has no estimate of arable available to the
average peasant household. It appears that the 'full peasant
stead' [*polnyi dvor*] is usually said to have had at its disposal
6 dessiatines (1 dessiatine equals 2.7 acres) of arable land
(cf. V. O. Kliuchevskii, *Sochineniya, op. cit.* Vol. IV, p. 145). The
contemporaneous average yield of rye as given by Strumilin
(p. 144) amounted to 34.9 pood per dessiatine. An earlier
source (E. I. Indova, in *Ocherki istorii Rossii, Period feodalisma,
op. cit.* p. 50) gives a higher yield. She claims that for European Russia of the period 2 *chetverti* (1 *chetvert'* equalled 8.6
pood) of rye seeds were used per 1 dessiatine, the yield being
on an average, according to Strumilin, three times higher
than the seeds (p. 157). This would give a good deal higher
yield of 51.6 pood per dessiatine (8.6 times 2 times 3). Let us
assume that the actual average yield was in between Strumilin's and Indova's estimates, amounting to 43.2 pood (34.9
plus 51.6 divided by 2). This yield must be diminished by
one-third to take account of seed requirements leaving a net
yield per dessiatine of 28.8 pood, which may or may not
include threshing losses. Applying this yield first to the 2
dessiatines of the field under winter grain, *i.e.* rye (under the
three-field system) gives a net yield from that field of 57.6
pood. The yield of the second field under spring grains was
somewhat lower according to Strumilin (33.4 pood per dessiatine, p. 144) and to a large part it was planted to oats. But
let us assume that the yields were identical in the 2 fields and
that three-quarters of the harvest could be used for human
consumption, the balance needed to maintain the draft power

of the farm in supplementing the inadequate winter storage of hay. On these assumptions, the yield from the second field would amount to 43.2 pood (57.6 times 0.75). (The assumption of equal yields no doubt involves an exaggeration as about double volume of oat seeds was planted per dessiatine, but the harvest was likely to yield less than the double volume of the seeds.) The total availability of grain for human consumption from the two fields (the third field, of course, lying fallow) would amount to 100.8 pood. Strumilin assumes that a peasant household consisted of 5 'male souls' (p. 328) or roughly 10 members. For the turn of the first decade of the eighteenth century (1710–11), Strumilin says that the aggregate tax collections per household in money and in kind amounted to 10 rubles in some cases and rose as high as 15 or even 16 rubles in others (p. 325). Kliuchevskii (*ibid.*) quotes a contemporary source for 1607 as assuming that a burden of 16 rubles per household was general. Assuming that the burden was somewhat diminished after the battle of Poltava, let us fix the tax burden for the period at 12.5 rubles per household.

The question then is: what quantity of grain was the equivalent of 12.5 rubles? Strumilin, anxious to show the high real wage of labor in Petrine Russia, makes much of the price for rye flour in the Urals (for 1720–9) which he says was 6.5 kopeks (0.065 rubles) per pood (p. 85). But this price (which would have to be further reduced to arrive first at the price for rye grain and then at the farmer's price) is obviously too low. In Olonets, the infertile region in the north (some 100 miles north-east of St Petersburg), the price was much higher, amounting in 1720 to 23 kopeks per pood of rye (p. 338). This price is obviously too high, but let us reduce it only to 20 kopeks per pood. At that price 12.5 rubles of tax collections would be the equivalent of 62.5 pood of grain, leaving the household with 38 pood of grain (100.8 minus 62.5). Since 1 pood equals 36.11 pounds (avoirdupois), 38 pood equal 1,370 pounds, this being the annual supply of basic foodstuff at the disposal of the household; or about 3.7 pounds per family and day (1,370 divided by 365). Since we assumed with Strumilin the household to consist of 10 persons, this means a daily ration per person of just over one-third of a pound or about 6 ounces. Thus making rather conservative assumptions leads to the conclusion that the peasant during Peter's reign disposed of a supply of grain which implied a disastrously low calorific availability of what naturally was the staple item of the diet.

It may be added that in addition to other conservative assumptions, the foregoing calculation was also based on the assumption that the peasant household performed labor services [*barshchina*] for the seignor [*pomeshchik*], but neither paid quitrent nor was under obligations to make any deliveries in kind to the *pomeshchik*.

How conservative the foregoing assumptions have been, is shown by the fact that Strumilin himself in another study says that in 1714 around Moscow a *chetvert'* of rye flour (not rye grain) cost 1 ruble or 11.6 kopeks per pood, as against the price of 20 kopeks used above. Furthermore, with regard to estimating the weight of the tax burden falling on the harvest from the second field (spring grains), note that as late as 1720 in Olonets the price of a pood of oats amounted to only 11.6 kopeks and must have been still lower in the central regions of the state. Cf. S. G. Strumilin, *Istoriya chernoy metallurgii v S.S.S.R.*, Vol. I, *Feodal'nyi Period, 1500–1680* [History of Ferrous Metalmaking in the U.S.S.R., Feudal Period] (Moscow, 1954), p. 143.

One can only say that what prevented the peasantry's wholesale death from starvation must have been: 1) the fact that some of the taxation in kind consisted in labor services supplied in the winter months when the labor force was otherwise unutilized; and 2) the limited quantity of products other than grain that were available to the peasants.

26   p. 75. S. G. Strumilin, *Ocherki, op. cit.* p. 286.

27   p. 76. V. O. Kliuchevskii, *op. cit.* Vol. IV, p. 126.

28   p. 76. It is fair to note, however, that not all Soviet historians take as complacent a view of the peasantry's 'ruination' as does Strumilin. Cf. *e.g.* A. M. Pankratova, *Formirovanie proletariata v Rossii, XVII-XVIII vekov* [Formation of the Proletariat in Russia in the 17th and 18th centuries] (Moscow, 1963) Chap. 9, pp. 320-58.

29   p. 76. *Polnoe sobranie zakonov Rossiyskoy Imperii* [Complete Collection of Laws of the Russian Empire], Vol. 5 (St Petersburg, 1830), Number 3203: 10 (May 1718), p. 571.

30   p. 76. 'Sotsial'nyi sostav rabochikh pervoy poloviny XVIII veka' ['The Social Composition of Workers in the First Half of the 18th Century'], in Akademiya Nauk S.S.S.R., Trudy istorico-arkheograficheskogo instituta, *Krepostnaya manufaktura v Rossii* [Serfdom Manufactory in Russia] (Leningrad, 1934), Pt IV, p. xv.

31   p. 76. V. O. Kliuchevskii, *op. cit.* Vol. IV, p. 118; *Polnoe sobranie zakonov Rossiyskoy Imperii.* Vol. 5 (St Petersburg,

1830), Number 2876 (January 1715), p. 137. For Peter's stress on compulsion in creating entrepreneurs and for his comparison of the entrepreneurs with children that must be forced, cf. *Polnoe sobranie zakonov Rossiyskoy Imperii*, Vol. 7 (St Petersburg, 1830), Number 4345 (November 1723), p. 150.

32 p. 77. As is usual in such debates, there has been also an attempt to establish a compromise solution. Professor Druzhinin has argued that the Petrine enterprises were 'capitalist' with regard to productive forces and 'feudal' with regard to 'production relations'. Unfortunately, to force an 'un-Marxian' situation into the mold of Marxian terminology is not very illuminating. Cf. N. M. Druzhinin, 'Sotsial'no-ekonomicheskie usloviya obrazovaniya Russkoy burzhuaznoy natsii' ['The Socio-Economic Conditions of the Formation of the Russian Bourgeois Nation'], in *Voprosy formirovaniya russkoy narodnosti i natsii, Sbornik statey* [Problems of Formation of Russian Nationality and Nation, A Collection of Essays] (Moscow–Leningrad, 1958), p. 206.

33 p. 77. Cf. F. Ya. Polyanskii, 'Lecture Seven', in *Istoriya narodnogo khozyaystva S.S.S.R. Kurs lektsii* [History of the National Economy of the U.S.S.R. A Course of Lectures] (Moscow, 1960), p. 128; *Polnoe sobranie zakonov Rossiyskoy Imperii*, Vol. 5 (St Petersburg, 1830), Number 3140 (January 1718), p. 530.

34 p. 78. D. Baburin, *Ocherki po istorii manufaktur-kollegii* [Essays in the History of the Manufacture-Collegium] (Moscow, 1939), p. 67.

35 p. 78. A. M. Pankratova, *op. cit.* p. 329; E. V. Spiridonova, *Ekonomicheskaya politika i ekonomicheskie vzglyady Petra I* [Economic Policy and Economic Views of Peter I] (Moscow, 1957), p. 204.

36 p. 78. P. N. Miliukov, *Gosudarstvennoe khozyaystvo . . ., op. cit.* p. 369.

37 p. 78. S. G. Strumilin, *Ocherki, op. cit.* (edition: Moscow, 1966) p. 344.

38 p. 79. Friedrich Engels, *Der Ursprung der Familie, des Privateigentums und des Staates*, in Karl Marx und Friedrich Engels, *Ausgewaehlte Schriften*, Vol. II (Berlin, 1955), p. 298. In fact, Engels's equilibrium theory is an elaboration of a thought expressed by Marx in one of his very early writings: 'Modern historiography has demonstrated how the absolute monarchy appears in the transitional period in which the old feudal estates are declining and the estate of medieval bur-

148

gesses is in the process of becoming the class of modern bourgeoisie; without either one of the warring parties being able to defeat the other. Thus the elements upon which the absolute monarchy is built, are by no means its product. They are rather its social pre-condition.' Cf. Karl Marx, 'Die moralisierende Kritik und die kritisierende Moral', in Karl Marx–Friedrich Engels, *Werke* (Berlin, 1859), Vol. 4, p. 346. Whatever the validity of this attempt to salvage the class theory for the relevant periods in the West, it patently breaks down when applied to Russian history. It is, incidentally, curious that Engels, despite his theory did not hesitate once to describe Napoleon I as 'the creator of the German bourgeoisie'. (Friedrich Engels, 'Der Status quo in Deutschland', in Marx–Engels, *Werke, op. cit.* p. 45.) Soviet historians will hardly be willing to draw the obvious and powerful inference *a fortiori*. It might be added that a more reasonable application of the concept of 'equilibrium of class forces' was made by Otto Bauer in *Die oesterreichische Revolution* (Vienna, 1923), pp. 243 ff. But in Bauer's hands the concept was applied to the democratic government in Austria in the early period of the First Republic and was not designed to explain the origins of a dictatorship. When, finally, a dictatorial government was established in Austria, no one could claim that it had emerged from an 'equilibrium' situation. It is true, of course, that even in this case 'equilibrium' defined any precise measurement. But at least one knew what was supposed to equal what, which is more than one can say of the very loose concept of equilibrium in some modern sociological works.

39   **p. 80.** E. I. Zaozerskaya, 'Begstvo i otkhod krest'yan v pervoy polovine XVIII veka' ['Flight and Temporary Migration of the Peasants in the First Half of the 18th Century'], in *K voprosu o pervonachal'nom nakoplenii v Rossii XVII-XVIII vekov* [On the Question of Original Accumulation in Russia in the 17th and 18th Centuries] (Moscow, 1958), pp. 145-88.

40   **p. 81.** Cf. R. Van der Meulen, *Nederlandse Woorden in het Russisch; Verhandelingen der Koninklijke Nederlandse Akademie van Wetenschappen*, Afdeling Letterkunde, New Series, Pt 64: 2 (Amsterdam, 1959); Van der Meulen, *Hollandse Zee en Schepstermen in het Russisch* (Amsterdam, 1909); N. A. Smirnov, *Zapadnoe vliyanie na russkii yazyk v petrovskuiu epokhu* [Western Influences on the Russian Language during the Petrine Epoch] (St Petersburg, 1910).

41   **p. 81.** V. O. Kliuchevskii, *Sochineniya* [Works] (Moscow, 1958), Vol. IV, p. 130.

42 p. 82. S. A. Pokrovskii, *Vneshnyaya torgovlya i vneshnyaya torgovaya politika Rossii* [Russia's Foreign Trade and Foreign Commercial Policy] (Moscow), 1947, pp. 84-7; K. Lodyzhenskii, *Istoriya russkago tamozhennago tarifa*, Prilozhenie [History of the Russian Customs Tariff, Appendix] (St Petersburg, 1886).

43 p. 83. I. T. Pososhkov, *Kniga o skudosti i bogatstve* [Book on Poverty and Wealth], ed. B. B. Kafengauz (Moscow, 1951).

44 p. 83. A. I. Pashkov, 'Ideolog kupechestva I. T. Pososhkov i ego *Kniga o skudosti i bogatstve*' ['The Ideologue of the Merchants, I. T. Pososhkov and his *Book on Poverty and Wealth*'], in *Istoriya russkoy ekonomicheskoy mysli* [History of Russian Economic Thought] (Moscow, 1955), Vol. I, Chap. 12, p. 361; also: B. B. Kafengauz, *I. T. Pososhkov, Zhizn' i deyatel'nost'* [I. T. Pososhkov, Life and Activity] (Moscow, 1951), p. 101; Kafengauz, being a much more serious scholar, is somewhat more restrained than Pashkov in his praise of Pososhkov.

45 p. 84. Since food was indeed the most important weight losing input in the industry of the time (with the exception, of course, of the production of ferrous metals), Pososhkov's suggestion was not necessarily irrational and must be judged in terms of the importance to be attached to the advantages stemming from agglomeration. The medieval cities in the West never would have become the centers of industrial activities if the advantages of agglomeration in the broadest sense possible had not far outweighed the pull of the costs of food.

46 p. 84. Cf. Eli F. Heckscher, *An Economic History of Sweden* (Harvard University Press, 1954), pp. 120-4.

47 p. 84. I. T. Pososhkov, *op. cit.*, pp. 177-8.

48 p. 84. I. T. Pososhkov, *op. cit.* p. 177.

49 p. 85. Computed from Strumilin, *Ocherki, op. cit.* p. 341.

50 p. 86. Adam Smith, *An Inquiry into the Nature and Causes of the Wealth of Nations* (Modern Library Edition, New York, 1937), p. 460.

51 p. 86. Adam Smith, *op. cit.* (London, 1864, p. 201).

52 p. 89. Arnold Luschin von Ebengreuth, *Grundriss der oesterreichischen Reichsgeschichte* (Bamberg, 1918), p. 369.

LECTURE 4

1 p. 97. C. H. Feinstein (ed.), *Socialism, Capitalism, and Economic Growth, Essays Presented to Maurice Dobb* (Cambridge University Press, 1967).

2 **p. 97.** E. H. Carr, 'Some Random Reflections on Soviet Industrialization', *op. cit.* pp. 271-84.

3 **p. 98.** Alexander Gerschenkron, *Economic Backwardness in Historical Perspective* (Harvard University Press, 1962); and *Continuity in History and Other Essays* (Harvard University Press, 1968).

4 **p. 100.** I must point out that this conversion of necessary and sufficient *conditions* in a definition into necessary and sufficient *preconditions* in a historical process (which smuggles the metaphysical concept of necessity into historical work) is at best a coarse analogy and actually a sleight of hand.

5 **p. 101.** Karl Marx, *Das Kapital*, Vol. i, Chap. 24.

6 **p. 105.** Edward Hallett Carr, *What is History?* (New York, 1962).

7 **p. 106.** The last phrase in the text calls for a qualification. For I *am* beginning to get nostalgic about that wonderful decade 1954–64, when the academic freedom at American universities was in no danger of being destroyed either by Rightists or by Leftists. But this nostalgia certainly has no bearing on my disagreements with Professor Carr.

8 **p. 108.** It is another matter that such sailings upstream, against the current of history, may prove rather hazardous, the desired destination of such trips being quite uncertain. This was well demonstrated by Wassily Leontief in his article, 'When should History be Written Backward?', *The Economic History Review*, Second Series, Vol. xvi, No. 1 (August 1963), pp. 1-8.

9 **p. 110.** Henri Monnier, *Les Mémoires de Monsieur Joseph Prudhomme* (Paris, 1857), Vol. i, pp. 46-67.

10 **p. 112.** E. H. Carr, 'Random Reflections . . .' *op. cit.* pp. 281-2.

11 **p. 114.** Eric Dahmén, *Svensk industriell företagarverksamhet* (Stockholm, 1950), Vol. i, p. 70.

12 **p. 116.** Cf. *e.g.* A. I. Pashkov, *Ekonomicheskii zakon preimushchesvennogo rosta proizvodstva sredstv proizvodstva* [Economic Law Concerning the Faster Growth of Output of Producers' Goods] (Moscow, 1958). Pashkov's thesis, a pseudo-scholarly elaboration of Khrushchev's political pronouncements at the time, is a curious Soviet version of Mr Micawber's rule: If the annual rate of growth of producers' goods is 8% and the rate of growth of consumers' goods is 7.5%, this means economic development, industrial progress, and eventually the advent of communism. If the two rates are reversed, this means stagnation, decay, and perhaps collapse of planned economy.

13 p. 118. Alexander Gerschenkron, *Continuity in History, op. cit.* Chap. 11.

14 p. 119. E. H. Carr, 'Random Reflections . . .', p. 273.

15 p. 119. E. H. Carr, 'Random Reflections . . .', p. 274.

16 p. 119. E. H. Carr, *What is History?*, p. 194.

17 p. 120. E. H. Carr, 'Random Reflections . . .', p. 282.

18 p. 123. Henry Adams, *The Education of Henry Adams* (Boston, 1918), pp. 409-10: 'Ten or fifteen years of violent stimulus seemed resulting in nothing.' Also: Henry Adams, *Letters*, ed. W. C. Ford (Boston–New York, 1938), p. 344.

19 p. 127. E. H. Carr, *What is History?*, pp. 126-8.

INDEX

(Prepared by Margarita Willfort)

154

155